12-16 years

37481

CC 1986

D0934332

DATE DUE

37481

Books by Richard B. Lyttle

PEOPLE OF THE DAWN
Early Man in the Americas

WAVES ACROSS THE PAST
Adventures in Underwater Archeology

THE GAMES THEY PLAYED
Sports in History

The Games
They
Played

RICHARD B. LYTTLE

The Games They Played

Sports in History

ILLUSTRATED BY THE AUTHOR

Atheneum 1982 New York

LIBRARY OF CONGRESS CATALOGING IN PUBLICATION DATA

Lyttle, Richard B.
The games they played.

Bibliography: p. 141
Includes index.
SUMMARY: Examines archeological evidence that reveals
how individual and team sports and games
have been used for diversion since prehistory.
1. Games—History—Juvenile literature. 2. Sports—
History—Juvenile literature. [1. Games—History—Juvenile
literature. 2. Sports—History] I. Title.
GV1200.L93   794   82-1749
ISBN 0-689-30928-7   AACR2

Published simultaneously in Canada by
McClelland & Stewart, Ltd.
Composition by
American–Stratford Graphic Services, Inc., Brattleboro, Vermont
Printed and bound by
Fairfield Graphics, Fairfield, Pennsylvania
Designed by Mary M. Ahern
First Edition

This book is for
MARTY ROSSMAN

C O N T E N T S

INTRODUCTION

Can we survive without athletic games?

By definition, play time is nonproductive time. With the exception of the professional athlete, no one plays to buy groceries or pay the rent. In fact, you might think that if we stopped playing so much and devoted more time to business all of us would be a lot better off.

But it's not true.

Play is a human necessity. This book, which describes just a few of the more popular, ancient sports, shows that people have played all through the ages. If we tried to describe all the games they played, including card, dice and board games as well as athletic contests, the book would be too heavy to carry.

Humans are not alone in their need for play. Recent studies show that the play of young animals is vital for their normal development. Therefore, its not surprising that tracing the origin of games can run into difficulty. Some games may be older than man himself.

In light of the importance of play, it is strange that serious study of games has only recently begun. We still have a great deal to learn about the relationship between sports and past cultures and between sports and the future of civilization.

Games and our attitude toward them might well influence the future. Much has been said, for instance, of sports as an outlet for aggression. It was even suggested for a time that sports might prevent wars. The idea was that the energy needed for war could be diverted to the playing field where it could escape like steam from a safety valve.

The notion turned out to be false. In fact, you will find in these pages a strong suggestion that the reverse might be true. High interest in sports, particularly combat sports, may indicate aggressive natures and a society that is likely to go to war.

There is much more food for thought in the study of ancient games. Just compare the Greeks and Romans. The Greeks were a nation of athletes. The Romans were a nation of spectators. The Greeks excelled in philosophy and the arts. The Romans were great engineers and master politicians. Both were aggressive, but the Greeks wasted much of their energy fighting each other, while the Romans used their aggressive energy to build an empire.

Many games, such as the Mayan court game, were founded in religious ritual. The Maya were a relatively peaceful people, but the Toltecs and the Aztecs who followed were bloodthirsty. The Toltecs and the Aztecs played the same court game, but its religious importance had been forgotten.

And what about team sports? Do they really promote cooperative societies? We don't yet know.

It is difficult to draw any firm conclusions on the relationships between sports and societies because we still have much more to learn.

If this book sparks your interest, it will have filled its purpose. With an increased interest in the relationship of society and games, perhaps this knowledge will one day show us a past that is more clearly understood and a future with a brighter promise.

P A R T I

Individual
Sports

Chapter One

To Honor the Gods

Here where two rivers met, a grove of wild olives gave rare shade on the sun-drenched plain. It was a resting place for the early migrants.

These migrants came to Greece from the north. A long march brought them to the Gulf of Corinth. Another long march took them around this gulf into the Peloponnesus, the southernmost territory of the Greek peninsula.

The little bands of tired travelers then had a choice. They could climb the mountains that faced them or they could work westward to the broad plain that sloped down to the Ionian Sea. The plain offered an easy route into the Peloponnesus. Most migrants took the easy way, and it brought them to the place where the wild olives grew.

It was an ideal camping spot. The two rivers, the west-running Alpheios and the smaller Kladeios that ran down from the north, gave plenty of fresh water even in the dry season. And the trees offered more than just shade.

From the dawn of time, primitive people have worshiped trees, and this cluster of olives soon became known as a sacred grove. Here the migrants gave thanks to their gods and prayed for safe travel in the days to come.

The smoke of sacred fires rose through the branches. Fruits and animals were offered in sacrifice. Temples honoring all the important gods soon stood in the shade of the trees, and the place was given a name. It was called Olympia, and the land around it became known as Elis.

We know little about the early travelers who camped and prayed at Olympia before moving on, but old legends tell of one man who settled in Elis and made it his kingdom.

He was Pelops, and he became so famous that the territory of southern Greece, the Peloponnesus, was named in his honor. There were many stories about him, but the favorite story tells how he won his kingdom.

When he arrived in Elis the land was ruled by Oinomaios, a cruel king who held all his possessions with a jealous hand. His prize possession was his beautiful daughter, Hippodameia, and the king guarded her with a passion.

He had good reason to guard her, for according to the legend, Oinomaios had been warned by an oracle that he would be killed by his son-in-law. So, as long as the maid never married, the king believed he would escape this fate.

The girl's beauty, however, attracted suitors in swarms. Oinomaios, forced to deal with them, devised a cruel plan.

He said that the man who could beat him in a chariot race would win his daughter's hand. But anyone who accepted his challenge and lost would be beheaded.

As a charioteer, the king had no master, and he owned the fastest horses in the land. Just the same, his challenge was accepted by thirteen suitors. All of them were beaten by the king. All of them died.

Pelops became the fourteenth suitor to accept the challenge. Hippodameia, perhaps for love but more probably out of boredom, hoped that her father would at last be beaten, but there was nothing she could do to help the brave Pelops.

He had to devise his own strategy. Pelops, a realist, knew he could not beat the king in a fair race. So the night before the contest, he went secretly to the royal stables where he bribed a groom to weaken the axle of the king's chariot.

This threw the odds in Pelops' favor, but Oinomaios, unaware of the treachery, rode out on the plain next day full of confidence. And the moment the race began, he took the lead as usual.

But suddenly the weakened axle broke. The king fell, became tangled in the traces, and was dragged to death by the frightened horses.

Winning both Hippodameia and the kingdom, Pelops ordered a funeral for the dead king. It turned into a festival of dancing, singing, prayers of thanks, and a variety of athletic competitions. And this, the legend says, was how the Olympic games began.

There is, however, a similar legend that credits the famous games to Hercules, not Pelops. Son of the god Zeus and the mortal Alcmena, Hercules was a painful annoyance to Hera, Zeus's jealous wife. Hoping to destroy him, Hera forced Hercules to perform twelve desperate labors. Cleaning the Augean stables was one of these chores.

The stables, owned by king Augeus of Elis, had housed three thousand oxen for thirty years without ever being cleaned. Hercules did the job in one day simply by diverting the river Alpheus so it flowed through the stables and washed them out.

The king, angry with the way in which the job was

accomplished, rashly challenged Hercules to a fight. Hercules killed the king, gained a kingdom, and celebrated his victory with a funeral festival of games.

According to some versions of the story, Hercules actually revived games that Pelops had started. Sorting fact from fiction in legends is an exercise of guesswork, but we do have bits of information that suggest a historical base for these legends.

Pelops was real. A king by that name did rule well enough to be long remembered in southern Greece. And he may well have gained his kingdom by deposing a tyrant.

We also know that the early Indo-European people who migrated into Greece had a funeral tradition that called for footraces and other athletic contests. The tradition survived into historical times in both Europe and Siberia.

The first account of this funeral tradition bears attention. It is also the first and one of the finest examples of sports writing in world literature. It is found in Homer's *Iliad*. No one can say exactly when the great poet lived, but the Trojan War on which he based his epic occurred in about 1200 B.C.

After the Greeks and the Trojans had been at war on the plains of Ilium for several months, Homer tells us that the young Greek Patroclus fell in battle. Achilles ordered a hero's funeral with athletic competition to please the gods and do honor to Patroclus' spirit.

Prizes were offered, but they were hardly necessary to spark interest. The Greeks, weary of battle, welcomed any diversion, and the chance to race chariots, run footraces, box, wrestle, and engage in contests of arms was greeted in holiday spirit.

The first and most important event was the chariot race. Before the start, one of the contestants, Antilochus, received some advice from Nestor, his wise, old father. Skill, Nestor told his son, is more important than speed.

"One man will leave too much to his chariot and pair, letting them wander hither and thither over the track, foolishly letting them make a wide turn. Another may be driving mediocre horses, but he always keeps his eye on the turning post and he wheels close in; he does not forget to hold his beasts firmly by the oxhide reins and he watches the man ahead of him."

Nestor, in short, is telling his son to use his head.

During the race, Antilochus talks to his horses, warning them of Nestor's anger should they lose. But the warning does not help. Antilochus falls behind leaving Diomedes and Eumelus to battle for the lead. As the chariots dashed toward the finish Eumelus calls upon Apollo for help while Diomedes appeals to Athena.

Homer tells how the gods respond. Apollo makes the whip fall from Diomedes' hand. Athena retaliates by making Diomedes' horses run faster. Then, in the final dash, Athena breaks the yoke holding Eumelus' team. His chariot flips. Eumelus rolls in the dust. And Diomedes wins the race.

The gods, it seems, were not content to be honored by competition. They had to become involved, but divine involvement reflected the beliefs of Homer's times. The gods were always present and they shaped human affairs.

In boxing, the strongman Epeius challenged all comers. Euryalus was the only one brave enough to come forward. Epeius looked on him with scorn and boasted:

"With one mighty blow I will tear this fellow's flesh to ribbons. Let his mourners gather around and be ready to carry him away when I have finished with him."

Homer describes the action. "They engage their powerful hands. Their jaws grind horribly; the sweat pours

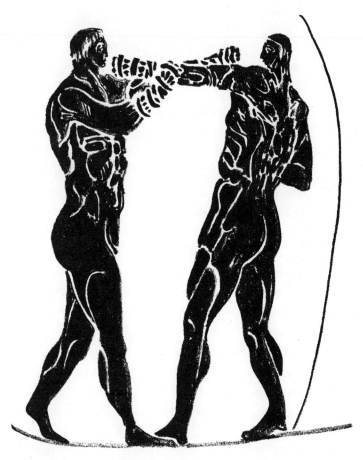

Although this vase painting dates back to the fourth century B.C., *it shows that Greek boxers were still using the thong bindings of Homer's time.*

down their limbs. Epeius hurls himself on his opponent, who casts a lost look about him as Epeius punches him on the jaw. Just as a fish is sometimes thrown on the shore by a gusty north wind and then is swamped by a black wave that covers him with seaweed, so Euryalus is cast head over heels on the ground."

It was a classic knockout punch. Epeius, a sportsman, tried to lift his opponent to his feet again, but Euryalus was out cold.

"His friends flock around him and conduct him across the ring with his legs dragging, his head lolling and his mouth spitting clots of blood."

With fists padded by nothing but oxhide bindings, boxing was a dangerous sport, and Homer knew it. Obviously, he had witnessed more than one bloody match.

In wrestling, Homer has Ajax and Ulysses, his two leading heroes, battle to a draw. Later, in armed combat, Ajax and Diomedes attack each other furiously. The fight becomes so heated that their friends, fearing serious injury or perhaps a fatal wound, pull the men apart and call an end to the contest.

The footrace becomes a contest again between Ajax and Ulysses. And once more, divine interference determines the outcome.

Ulysses asks Athena for help, and the goddess gives his legs extra speed. And just before the finish, she causes Ajax to trip and sprawl in cow dung.

A footrace depicted on a fifth century B.C. *vase shows the runners nearing the turning post on the left. The arm position and length of stride suggests a long distance race rather than a sprint.*

The winged goddess watching these wrestlers on a vase painting seems bored, but the painting illustrates the important belief that the gods watched when athletes performed.

The gods served Homer as a narrative device. When the gods intervened, his heroes were not disgraced. After all, a man could lose to the gods with no loss of dignity.

But Homer also wanted to praise the gods and illustrate their power. And most of all he wanted to show the religious aspect of sports, that athletic competition brought mortals closer to their gods. This was a keystone in the faith of ancient Greeks. It explains why Greece became a nation of athletes.

Of course, there was a practical benefit from competition. In a land where tribes and the city-states that evolved from them were almost constantly at war, physical fitness was vital. A man could be called upon to fight at any time and on short notice.

Those who could not run swiftly, throw a stone or spear with force, or defend themselves stoutly in hand-to-hand combat were of little use to their fellow citizens. Fitness and good health were respected simply because they were marks of good citizenship. And the best way to keep fit was to compete.

No city or town of any consequence in ancient Greece was without some kind of sports festival. There were hundreds of local festivals open to the citizens of the district only. At first, the festival at Olympia was no different from others.

The story of its evolution into a national festival, the longest uninterrupted event in the history of sports, is a matter of record.

Chapter Two

To Come in Peace

Ownership of Olympia was disputed. Did the sacred grove where the two rivers joined belong to the Eleans or their neighbors, the Pisatans? As the importance of Olympia as a place of worship and games increased so did the heat of the dispute.

Angry words were followed by blows. Then came full war.

We don't know how long the fighting went on, but we can assume that as long as the Eleans and the Pisatans remained enemies, neither could enjoy the pleasure of visiting Olympia.

Wisdom eventually prevailed. A truce was established giving the people of both states the right to use the shrine on one important condition. All must come unarmed. Olympia would henceforth be a place of peace.

The terms of the truce between the Eleans and the

Pisatans were inscribed in a bronze discus that was dated 776 B.C. Unfortunately, the discus has been lost, but it apparently was still on display at Olympia in 175 A.D. when Pausanias, a traveler and author, saw it and described it in one of his books.

Although a local festival had been held previously at Olympia for untold years, the historical beginning of the Olympic Games is set at the year of the truce—776 B.C. The games continued on a four-year cycle until 393 A.D., a span of almost twelve centuries. No other event in sports has lasted so long.

Strict enforcement of the truce helped the games endure, but there was another agreement made about the time of the truce that gave lasting strength to the spirit of competition. While a local festival, valuable prizes, including decorated vases filled with wine or olive oil, had been awarded the victorious athletes. Soon after the truce, however, the prizes were replaced by a crown of olive branches cut from the sacred grove.

Having no material value, the crown symbolized the importance of excellence for its sake alone. This became the spirit of Olympic competition.

The crown also had religious significance. Branches for it had to be cut with a golden knife by a boy whose parents were still living. We don't know the significance of these requirements, but their strict enforcement leaves little question of their importance.

The olive crown set the games apart from other festivals. The Olympic games became something special. Athletes from other neighboring states were soon competing at Olympia.

Sparta, long a troublesome neighbor, made truce so its athletes could compete. Within fifty years, the games beside the sacred grove were drawing athletes from through-

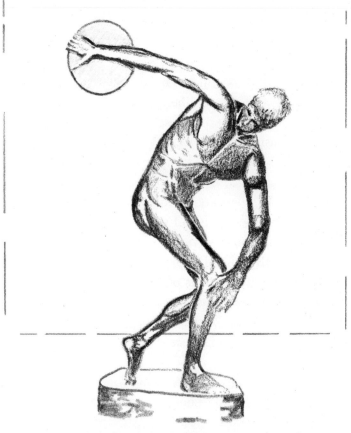

Only two copies of statues by the fifth century B.C. *sculptor Myron have survived. One of them is his discus thrower, a study in power and balance.*

out the Pelopennesus. And a hundred years after the Elean-Pisatan truce, Athens and Greek colonies on the eastern shores of the Aegean were taking part.

It was Sparta, however, that dominated the competition during this period of expansion, and Spartan athletes added two lasting traditions. They competed in the nude and they used oil to clean their bodies.

There was no shame associated with nudity. The unclad body prompted pride and admiration, and bare limbs in action inspired poetry and some of the most extraordinary statues the world has ever known.

The bath of olive oil was a two step procedure. The athlete first spread the oil liberally on his body. Then he scraped it away with a curved stick. Because the Spartans were such consistent winners, it was thought that the oil bath imparted magical power, and the oil bath quickly became a tradition among all Greek athletes. Actually, the only real benefit was a cooling and cleansing of the skin.

The price of cleansing oil was often the major cost in financing a community's gymnasiums, so large flasks of oil were traditionally offered as prizes in local sports festivals. Fortunately for the students of Greek history, these prize flasks or amphora were usually decorated with scenes depicting various events of the festivals. In many cases they provide the only pictorial record of competition that has survived.

At Olympia, the variety of events increased with the ever-growing number of competitors. By some accounts, the games began with a footrace for boys. The fastest youth won the right to take a torch from a priest and light a fire before Zeus's altar.

This story, however, seems to conflict with the legend and tradition of a variety of games as part of funeral rites. We do know that after 776 B.C. new events were constantly being added, and the festival, at first a one day affair, eventually took five days.

Hippias of Elis, who lived in the fifth century B.C. and compiled a list of early Olympic winners, reported that the two-stad footrace, a distance of some one thousand feet, was added in 714 B.C. A long-distance race, length unknown, was added in 720 B.C. And the pentathlon was added in 708 B.C. This was the first combination event, testing excellence in running, jumping, wrestling, and the discus and javelin throws.

In 680 B.C., Hippias' list reveals that the four-horse

The javelin-thrower's style is well illustrated by a fifth century B.C. *vase painting. Post at right apparently marked the throwing line.*

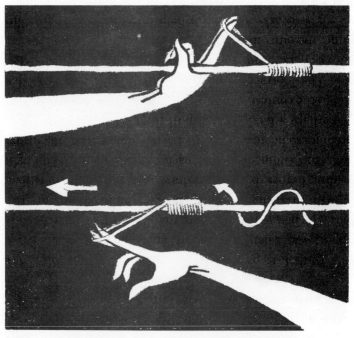

Close study of the vase painting showed scholars how the athlete used a thong to make the shaft spin. A spinning javelin gave an accurate throw, and accuracy was the main goal in the early Olympic version of the sport.

chariot race was introduced, perhaps replacing races with two-horse teams. In 648 B.C. horse racing and the brutal pankration were added. Pankration combined boxing and wrestling with few holds barred. Only biting and eye-gouging were illegal.

Foot races and wrestling for boys up to age eighteen were introduced in 616 B.C. Eventually, competition for boys in almost all events, including pankration, was offered.

Girls and women were not allowed to compete at Olympia, and married women were not even allowed to attend the games as spectators. There was, however, a special festival open to all unmarried women of Greek citizenship.

The man on top prepares to deliver a chopping blow to his opponent's back in a 300 B.C. statue of pankration. This drawing is based on the reconstruction of a badly broken copy of the original statue.

Modeled after the Olympics with an olive crown as the coveted prize, the festival honored Hera, wife of Zeus. The most popular event in the Heraea, as it was called, was apparently a footrace of about 500 feet.

Actually, it was the local festivals that offered the most opportunity for women athletes. In many of them, they were allowed to race and wrestle against boys. In some towns, it was the custom for girls to test the power of their suitors by running races against them. Just the same, it has to be said that most Greek states did not give women athletes equal status with men.

Sparta was the exception. There, girls and women were encouraged to train and take part in all competition open to boys. Spartan women attributed their good health and their beauty to their rigorous athletic training.

By the sixth century B.C., the Olympics had become so popular that several other sports festivals tried to change from local to national status. Just three made the transition successfully.

North of the Gulf of Corinth, the town of Delphi, home of the famous oracle, had been holding musical competitions on an eight-year cycle for many years. In 582 B.C. the festival was put on a four-year schedule and horse and chariot races and a variety of athletic events were added to the games. Valuable prizes were replaced by laurel crowns.

In the same year, a local festival held at Corinth was expanded to include all athletes of Greek citizenship. Musical competition, horse races, even a regatta were added to the program. The games at Corinth were held every other year.

Southwest of Corinth and east of Olympia, the town of Nemea soon switched its local festival to national status. A crown of parsley became the prize in the Nemean games, which were also held every other year.

A marble copy of a fifth century B.C. *bronze shows that the female athlete's attire was a loose-fitting dress worn off one shoulder. This runner is believed to be poised at her starting line.*

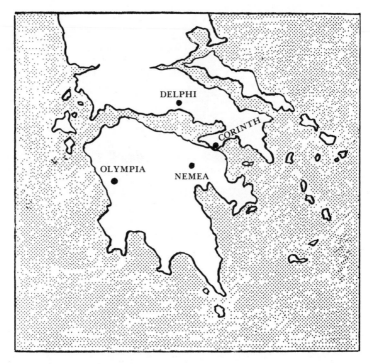

Spread across the heartland of Greece, the big four of sports festivals attracted competitors from distant colonies as well as city-states of the mainland.

The new festivals, with the Olympics, became the Big Four of competition. It was the ambition of every athlete to win the crown at each festival for a sweep, or in today's phrase, a grand slam of excellence. Those who did achieve this goal became national heroes.

An athlete, however, did not have to score a sweep to be honored in his home town with praise and awards. Although a crown of parsley or wild olive had no material value, many benefits were heaped upon returning heroes.

Some towns excused their winners from paying taxes for the rest of their lives. Others gave a lifetime of free meals, complimentary tickets to theaters, honored seats in the town senate or other governing body, or simply gifts of money. Honors were many and varied.

One town, so excited to have an Olympic winner, tore

down a section of wall so the hero could make a triumphant return through a gate never before used.

Odes were written in praise of heroes, and they were read at public gatherings held in their honor. Towns commissioned statues of their winners, and these statues were often placed in the shrines where the victory occurred. At Olympia, scores of statues of famous athletes shared the sacred ground with statues of the gods.

Because the games were inspired by the belief that competition honored the gods, cheating in any event was extremely rare. It was not uncommon, however, for an athlete to lie about his place of birth in order to increase his benefits from victory. Apparently, it was just being practical for a man born in a poor village to claim citizenship in a large city where the citizens could afford to be more generous.

By the fifth century B.C., Greece had become a nation of athletes. In the Greek mind, love of sports set the civilized man apart from the barbarian. This belief received a tremendous boost when the Persian wars concluded in 449 B.C. with Greek victory. A loose union of Greek states populated by free citizens had conquered oriental despotism. A handful of well-trained soldiers had beaten undisciplined hordes. Athletes had vanquished barbarians.

Sports festivals celebrated the victory and gave outlet for a new spirit of pride and accomplishment. Old shrines were rebuilt and new shrines were erected at Delphi, Corinth, Nemea, and Olympia. Philosophers, politicians, poets, minstrels, and artists as well as athletes jammed the festival grounds. The national games became national fairs.

Ambassadors settled differences and signed pacts. Often these documents were stored in one of the shrines on the festival grounds. Merchants displayed their goods and signed trade agreements. Artists showed off their latest

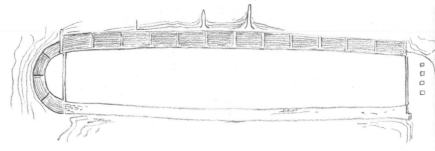

The stadium at Delphi, one of the best preserved, was 580 feet long, ninety-three feet wide at the middle, and eighty-three feet wide at either end. Square pillars on the right marked the starting line for footraces.

creations. Musicians introduced their new works. Philosophers argued theories and logic. Poets read their verses. Orators showed off their eloquence.

Anyone who wished to stay in the mainstream of Greek life was compelled to attend the national sports festivals. No one, however, attended these crowded affairs with much hope of personal comfort.

Olympia, never more than a small village, had only enough housing for priests and a few officials. Everyone else camped out. Because the five-day event was held in August, rain was rare, and with little shade, the summer heat could be merciless.

At their peak, the Olympic games attracted forty thousand spectators. Bathing was impossible, and in dry years even drinking water was scarce. Sometimes the stadium was so crowded there was no room to sit on the unbenched, sloping banks of the grandstand. And in reverence to the gods, hats were not permitted. Death from heatstroke was not uncommon.

After his visit to Olympia five hundred and fifty years after the Persian Wars, Epictetus, a first century A.D. writer, complained of the crowds, lack of water, and the heat. But most of all he detested the stench of sacrifice that drew clouds of flies to the shrine. In Epictetus' day there were seventy altars at Olympia, and with each receiving offerings of fruit and flesh, the smell must have been overpowering.

By Epictetus' time the Greek sports festival had seen many changes as had Greek political, economic, and spiritual life. And athletes themselves had changed.

Professionalism had arrived. It had begun to develop when the number of important national festivals increased. To do well in all of them, an athlete had to stay in training year-round. Most citizens, lacking the time and the money for such intensive preparation, became spectators.

Amateurs continued to compete successfully at local festivals limited to the citizens of a single state or city, but the national festivals became the business of full-time athletes.

Horse and chariot races long continued to attract amateurs, but because of the expense of breeding and training horses, these events appealed mainly to the rich.

The political decline of Greece did not affect the games as much as one might suppose. Individual states, continuing to fight over their differences, had undermined democratic rule in many areas. And the fighting, particularly the long struggle between Athens and Sparta, had also sapped Greek wealth. But political rulers, including the despots who replaced popular rule, recognized the unifying power of the games. The rulers encouraged their continuance and donated funds for new shrines and statues and improved stadiums.

When Philip of Macedonia united Greece under his rule, he appointed himself president of the games at Delphi and entered and won a horse race at Olympia. His victory was recorded on coins minted to commemorate the event.

The Olympic priests, however, were still able to maintain their power under Philip. When some of his soldiers violated the sacred truce of the festival, Philip was fined. He paid the penalty without protest.

Alexander the Great, Philip's son, regarded Olympia as the center of the Greek world, a world he expanded as far as India. Statues of Alexander and his family were placed among the shrines at Olympia, and it was there, in 324 B.C., that he ordered that the document declaring himself a god be read.

Self-proclaimed divinity, however, did not prevent an early death for Alexander, and with that death, Greek influence began to wane.

Colonies in the west fell under the dominance of Carthage or Rome. Athletes from the western colonies, once so numerous and successful, faded from competition. Very few made the long journey to Olympia and the other sports centers. Greek colonies to the east, however, thrived, and they continued to send their athletes to the homeland until well into the second century B.C.

By then, however, Rome had taken over most of the world that Alexander had conquered. Mainland Greece was impoverished both financially and in spirit. The games at Olympia might have come to an end had not the Romans recognized their benefit to Greek morale and their political possibilities.

Many a Roman emperor and governor won support from Greek cities and colonies by seeing that sports festivals continued and gymnasiums remained open. But Romans themselves were spectators not athletes.

To the practical Roman mind, stripping to the bare flesh and working up a sweat to win a prize that had no value was both silly and undignified. But the festivals kept the conquered people happy, and many Romans discovered that the games were great fun to watch.

Under Roman rule, sports festivals actually multiplied, but the nature of sports changed dramatically. Boxing, pankration, and chariot racing appealed to Romans for their value as spectacles. These events were stressed at the expense of running, jumping, and javelin throwing.

Augustus Caesar, whose rule from 27 B.C. to 14 A.D. brought unity and strength to the empire, was a great sports fan. He particularly liked boxing, but he encouraged all sports. He ordered coins minted to commemorate the Olympics and other famous festivals, and he established two new festivals, the Actium at Rome and the Augustus games at Naples. The Actium was almost a direct copy of the Olympic games, complete with wreaths for prizes.

But Augustus could not change the tastes of the average Roman citizen. Stress on blood sports increased. Instead of binding their fists with thongs, boxers now wore the cestus, a metal weapon that fit over the knuckles and bristled with sharp points. Every blow drew blood. Death ended many contests. The Romans also opened competition to slaves.

Athletes who were freemen no longer competed for the honor of their home towns or states. Instead, they became traveling professionals owing allegiance only to their trade. Many organized guilds, and some of these guilds held charters issued by the emperor himself.

Despite the vast changes in sports, the Olympic games through the years retained much of their original character, and they continued to draw large crowds. At the crossroads of the eastern and western worlds, Olympia also continued to be an important meeting place for the exchange of ideas and cultures.

Only after the invasion of the Goths in the third century A.D. did the decline begin. Historical records of the day make little mention of the games but they continued well into the Christian era.

It was Christianity that brought them to an end. In the creed of the new religion, nudity was sinful, and physical competition held in public was immoral.

In 393 A.D., Theodosius I, emperor of Constantinople, banned the games at Olympia. His edict, however, was not enforced. The games continued sporadically until 529 A.D. when Justinian I, ruler of the Byzantine empire, renewed the ban. He enforced it with vigor. The pagan temples were torn down. The idols were smashed. And the stadium at the place where the two rivers joined fell into ruins.

Revival of the Olympic games as we know them today was prompted by Pierre, Baron de Coubertin, a French author and educator, who believed that games modeled after the old Olympics would be an ideal way to unite students of the world in a peaceful gathering.

In 1894, he sent letters to sports groups in many different countries outlining his ideas. They were greeted with enthusiasm, and in 1896, the first modern Olympic games were held in Athens, Greece.

Lack of organization and spotty participation did not give much promise for the future at Athens or at the games that followed at Paris and then at St. Louis. But in 1908, with highly successful games held at London, the tradition was firmly reestablished.

In 1928, Coubertin received a Nobel Prize for his contribution to world peace, and today the Olympics continue as the major event for amateur athletes throughout the world.

Chapter Three

Wrestling

In the late 1930s in the ruins of Khafaje, a city that was built 5,000 years ago, archeologists came upon a bronze casting of two wrestlers. Khafaje, part of the early Sumerian kingdom, stood near present-day Baghdad in the Tigris River valley.

Dr. E. A. Speiser, the American archeologist who headed the Khafaje expedition, made two interesting points about the finds.

First, he noted that the casting and a stone carving of a boxing match were found close to an altar dedicated to the Sumerian god of fertility. The location suggests that boxing and wrestling matches may have been part of ancient religious rites.

Second, both works of art could have been modeled after modern athletes. Dr. Speiser concluded that the styles of both wrestling and boxing have changed very little since 3000 B.C.

Even though styles are similar, rules and scoring systems for wrestling have differed greatly in different regions of the world. While most matches start with the opponents

The true heavyweights of today are Japan's sumo wrestlers, some of whom tip the scales at 400 pounds. Their pushing contests follow a style begun some fifteen hundred years ago.

standing, one form of wrestling begins with them on hands and knees. Today the aim in most modern matches is to pin the opponent's shoulders to the mat, but this was not the common goal in ancient times.

For early Egyptian and Greek wrestlers, the idea was simply to throw the opponent to the ground. Sumo wrestlers of Japan, who follow a tradition begun fifteen hundred years ago, try to force the opponent out of the ring or off the mat. Because weight is an asset in holding position in the ring, professional sumo wrestlers are great eaters. Some of them weigh more than 400 pounds.

There were no weight classifications for wrestling in the early Olympics and other sports festivals of the day. Thus big men dominated the event, but because strength and agility were also needed to throw an opponent, excess fat could be a handicap for the Greek wrestler.

Today, it is difficult to reconcile the pankration, that boxing-wrestling combination, with the Greek character. While Romans loved a brutal spectacle, we like to think that the Greeks, who practiced harmony in thought, art, and sports would not invent a free-for-all battle that allowed kicking and scratching. Yet there can be no doubt that the Greeks not only invented but also enjoyed pankration. Since this is the way soldiers fought in hand-to-hand combat, perhaps pankration got its boost as good training for warfare.

Pankration or combat very much like it was once common in India, and natives of Ceylon, off the Indian coast, were still holding boxing-wrestling matches, known as *malla pora,* in colonial times. Each contestant wore a Roman-like cestus on one fist in these matches. It is impossible today to say if this sport was invented independently in the East or if perhaps it evolved from the influence of Alexander's armies on their eastern march in the fourth century B.C.

Other wrestling methods unique to the East, jujitsu and the closely related judo, with holds and throws that use the opponent's weight and strength against him, originated some three thousand years ago with no suggestion of western influence. There are, however, conflicting stories on the origin of jujitsu.

One version holds that jujitsu was developed during

the Chou Dynasty in China, which extended from the twelfth to third centuries B.C. when emperors put great emphasis on physical fitness among their soldiers. The techniques were passed on secretly only to those judged worthy of the art.

Another version traces the origin to Buddhists of Japan, Tibet, and China who developed jujitsu as a secret means of defense through some two thousand years of experiment and practice.

Still another account says that the art did not reach Japan until the Hideyoshi invasion of 1592 A.D.

Judo, most authorities agree, was invented in 1882 by Jigoro Kano, a Japanese jujitsu expert. By eliminating the dangerous holds of jujitsu, he established judo as a sport that has been received with ever-growing popularity throughout the world.

While weight classifications are followed in formal competition, it is possible for a small judo expert to throw a much larger opponent. This trait of the art adds much to the appeal of judo as a means of defense.

Points are scored in a judo match when one player throws the other with force, when one is held down for thirty seconds, or when one has to submit because of a choke or other hold. Players wear jackets loosely held with a belt, and the color of the belt is a sign of talent. A white belt is worn by beginners, a black belt by the experts. Various other colors are used for intermediate levels.

While judo is largely a sport of participation, Japan's sumo wrestling has gained great popularity as a spectator sport. Many of the huge wrestlers are popular heroes with as much notoriety as movie stars of the western world.

The sport rose from religious rites, and when begun some fifteen hundred years ago, opponents reportedly fought to the death. Now the aim is to use weight and lev-

The jackets worn in judo provide hand-holds for throws,
making it relatively easy, for those who know how, to handle
opponents much bigger than themselves.

erage to force the other man from a fifteen-foot ring or plat-
form. Much formal ceremony is still followed and a Shinto
priest usually serves as referee.

At the beginning of a match, the opponents face each
other and make threatening gestures. They clap their hands
and lift their huge legs. Then each returns to his corner

for a handful of salt. He throws the salt into the ring as an act of purification, but often the salt is aimed at the opponent as a challenge.

Similar rituals are part of the preliminary tradition for wrestlers in Egypt and India. Usually, after a silent prayer, an Egyptian wrestler will touch his forehead to the floor of the arena three times, and if the match is staged on sand, he will lift a handful of sand to his brow.

Then like the sumo wrestler, the Indian or Egyptian combatant slaps his hands or biceps as he faces his opponent and tries to intimidate him. To win the match, however, the aim, as in the western world, is to pin the other man's shoulders.

An Etruscan wall painting shows that traditions and holds, including the hammer lock, were being practiced in Italy before the Romans came to power.

No matter what form wrestling takes, it is clear that those who step in the ring are carrying on a very ancient and respected tradition.

Perhaps the most famous wrestler of all time, certainly the most famous Greek wrestler was Milon of Crotona. Stories of his fabulous strength are legendary.

One story has it that Milon began his first day of training for the Olympic games by carrying a newborn calf on his shoulders. As the calf grew, so did Milon's strength, so that when the animal reached full weight, the wrestler could still carry it.

It's difficult to believe, but Milon reportedly demonstrated his training technique before forty thousand spectators at Olympia by carrying a four-year-old heifer 538 yards. After putting the animal down, he reportedly felled it with one blow of his bare fist. Then, when the animal had been butchered and cooked, he ate it, all of it, finishing the meal before the day was over.

Stories about him have surely been exaggerated over the centuries, but we do know that Milon recorded his first Olympic victory in 540 B.C., the year he competed in boy's wrestling.

As an adult wrestler, he won the olive crown five times at Olympia. He was a six-time winner at Delphi, a nine-time winner at Nemea, and a ten-time winner at Corinth.

Milon made his last appearance at Olympia in 512 B.C. when he faced a young opponent by the name of Timasitheos in the final match. The young man, using his agility and speed to elude Milon's grasp, eventually tired the older man. Milon, at last exhausted, was forced to retire.

One of the Milon legends, however, tells of a defeat of another kind. During one of his long, daily walks, Milon was said to have met the shepherd Timormos, a huge man of tremendous strength.

It did not take long for the two to agree upon a test of strength. Timormos, selecting a large boulder on the grassy slope, wrapped his arms around it, plucked it from the ground and carried it a distance of sixteen yards.

It was then Milon's turn. He clasped the rock in his arms and flexed all his muscles. The rock would not budge. He tried again and again with no success. Finally, he had to admit that Timormos was the stronger man.

Unfortunately, the shepherd was a slave and could not compete in any of the sports festivals open at that time only to freeborn Greek citizens.

This tale again may be based more on invention than fact, but we do know that Crotona, Milon's place of birth, was a breeder of athletes. A Greek colony in the Gulf of Taranto at the southern tip of Italy, Crotona dominated the Olympics for much of the sixth century B.C.

The phrase "healthy as a Crotoniate" became as common at that time as our "healthy as an ox."

Crotona was also famous for its school of philosophy headed by the great thinker Pythagoras, father of geometry. Milon, who married Pythagoras' daughter, became one of his devoted followers. The philosopher preached the virtue of harmony in all things, and Milon apparently filled his years of retirement with comfortable harmony.

He was always happy, however, to demonstrate his strength, and there were times when his strength was needed. One day when a large party had gathered in Pythagoras' house, the roof started to fall. Milon jumped to his feet and braced his mighty arms against the key beams. After everyone had fled, he released the beams and let the house crash to the ground around him. Then he stepped from the rubble unscathed.

There are two versions of Milon's death. The one that seems closest to fact says that Milon was killed about 500 B.C. during an uprising against Pythagoras and his followers. We know that many Crotoniates were killed then and that the colony was too weak afterwards to continue dominating at Olympia. The last Crotoniate competed there in 480 B.C.

The other version of Milon's death is more romantic. While walking in the hills, the hero reportedly came upon a huge tree that a woodsman had felled and left partially split. Unable to resist a test of strength, Milon widened the split with his bare hands. When he opened the gap, however, the woodsman's wedges fell out of place. Then, as his strength ebbed, the split closed upon his hands, trapping him.

Friends did not find Milon until wolves had partially eaten his body.

Perhaps the most famous wrestling match in history pitted Henry VIII, King of England, against François I, King of France.

The match occurred during a diplomatic parley near Calais, which was then an English possession. The nobles and courtiers of both nations came together in pomp and splendor. Each side tried to outdo the other in show of wealth and pageantry.

The field where the two camps met was covered with so much tapestry and so many colorful tents, and the costumes worn were so rich in silk and ornament that the place became known as the Field of Gold.

Although the diplomatic mission failed to settle differences between France and England, everyone apparently had a good time. A spirit of festival was maintained with sporting events, including jousting and wrestling.

Chagrined when a team of French wrestlers beat an English team, King Henry challenged King François to a match. François accepted and the two stripped to their waists and came to grips in the ring.

The record is not clear on the outcome. Perhaps the two monarchs battled to a draw before their cheering nobles. The remarkable thing is that no one thought it unusual or undignified for royalty to wrestle.

A hundred years later, after England's James I had claimed the divine right of royalty, such a match would have been unthinkable.

Chapter Four

Boxing

Although boxing's origins go far back into prehistoric times, it has not always been as popular as wrestling.

There is no evidence from ancient Egypt to suggest great interest in boxing there. Residents of Crete, on the other hand, were avid boxing fans. Crete and Egypt had strong trade and political ties and much exchange of culture for many centuries, but boxing was popular with one people and not with the other.

It might have been that the violent nature of the sport was contrary to Egyptian religious beliefs.

We do know that Spartan athletes were not allowed to box at any of the sports festivals. The sport was banned to them because of a belief that it was unmanly to admit physical inability. The belief was incompatible with boxing rules of the day. Not fought by rounds, a match went on until one of the contestants was unable to continue. No Spartan could expose himself to such utter defeat.

Although Sparta did not support it, boxing became popular throughout other Greek states both as a sport and as a training exercise for soldiers.

*A fragment of a carving from Crete shows the bold stance of a
1600 B.C. boxer. Though the lines are faint, it appears that
Cretan boxers bound their hands and wrists with rawhide just
as Homer's heroes did.*

Rules of the day permitted head blows only. Body
punches were not allowed, but a man could hit his opponent when he was down. There were no weight classifications, and this made it a big man's sport.

Fighters trained by hitting bags filled with sand or fig
seeds. Strips of oxhide softened with animal fat protected
the fists. Statues and carvings from the fourth and fifth centuries B.C. show that these bindings often extended up the
fighter's arms as far as his elbows.

The hidebound fist could do plenty of damage, but

the sport was not bloody enough to suit later Roman fans. Hide thus gave way to the brutal cestus. This weapon at first was a metal strip fitted and bound over the knuckles, but soon a cestus with sharpened points was being used.

We can imagine that the Roman boxer fought with arms high and relied heavily on his defensive skills to survive. A man who could parry a blow and counter quickly with one of his own would probably have an advantage over the brawler. With the cestus, however, one blow could put a man out of action, blind him, or even kill him. Few boxers had long careers in the Roman ring.

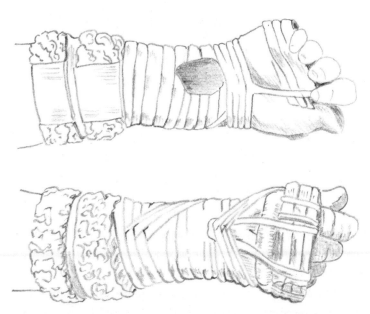

Both sides of the right hand of a boxer depicted in an Italian statue show how thongs were being wrapped and cut more to inflict damage on the foe that protect the hands. The trend led to the development of the cestus, a metal "protector" bristling with sharp points.

Understandably, few boxers of the day fought for the fun of it. Many were either slaves, compelled by their owners to risk their lives, or well-paid professionals.

With the fall of Rome boxing as a sport died out not to be revived until late in the 1500s when interest in sports of all kinds bloomed in England.

Running, jumping, fencing, wrestling, and boxing were pursued with enthusiasm. By 1620, with many professionals dominating these sports, plans were made for a huge sports amphitheater in London. Puritan objections killed the project, but a century later, with the monarchy restored, sports arenas were being constructed in all major cities.

Sports fans of the day were heavy bettors and they liked variety. Programs often included wrestling, boxing, sword, and cudgel fighting. Occasionally, women hacked at each other with swords.

When pleased by a performance, fans threw coins in the ring by the fistful. The money was gathered up and became part of the purse for the contestants.

Englishmen have always loved a good scrap, and it apparently did not take much to get one started. Stories are told of dock workers who would fight for a few shillings to entertain the swells waiting for a ferry boat. Good friends would go at each other in these barefisted bouts and fight until one of them could no longer stand. These were certainly exciting shows for the money.

But the times were right for James Figg, a man who could coax more money from the fight fans. A veteran of the boxing ring, Figg first began arranging bouts in 1719. Soon he launched an academy, what we would call a gym, for training young fighters.

His instruction in the "Noble Art of Self Defense" covered swordsmanship, cudgels, wrestling, and boxing.

As history's first fight promoter, Figg established the tradition of taking a healthy cut of the gate for himself and dividing the rest among the fighters. The winner got two thirds of the purse and the loser, one-third. He handled prefight publicity and advance ticket sales.

His arena on London's Oxford Street almost always had a full house on fight nights. At first, all forms of combat enjoyed equal popularity, but gradually boxing became the biggest attraction. Figg concentrated on boxing matches.

His most famous bout was an international affair staged in 1725 between Stopa l'Acqua, a giant of a man from Venice, Italy, and John Whitacker, Figg's best pupil.

L'Acqua, with a long record of victories, boasted that most of his victims had hit the canvas with broken jaws. Figg countered the boast with the claim that Whitacker's jaw was unbreakable. The prefight hoopla assured standing room only for the big event.

Actually, Whitacker's main asset was speed and agility. He was able to dodge, punch, and dance away from the heavy Italian. Finally, after the frustrated l'Acqua had begun to tire, Whitacker dropped him with a fierce body blow to end the fight.

Within hours of this bout, Figg began promoting another, saying that he had a man who could beat Whitacker in ten minutes. Again, he sold every seat in his gym for a fight between Whitacker and Nathaniel Peartree.

Peartree, a sharpshooter with his fists, did not find Whitacker an elusive target. Relentless blows to his head soon closed both Whitacker's eyes, forcing him to retire.

Although these bouts delighted the crowds and the heavy bettors, they were brutal for the fighters. Bare fists could cause serious injury, even death, but for many years, high risk was accepted as part of the sport.

The introduction of boxing gloves reduced much of the danger, but they were looked on by much of the sporting public as something only a sissy would wear. So even after bare-fisted fighting was outlawed in England, it continued on the sly in country towns and city suburbs.

Gentleman Jack Broughton changed all this. He wore gloves, but he was no sissy. He dominated the ring for ten years. His fighting career did not end until 1750, when he put his unbeaten record on the line against an unknown butcher by the name of Slack.

As usual, betting was heavy, and unfortunately King George the Second's son, the Duke of Cumberland, put ten thousand pounds on Gentleman Jack. When the champ lost, the duke was so angry that he forbade any mention of boxing in the royal house.

The sport, however, was too well established to suffer much damage from the loss of support by the nobility. Broughton, following Figg's example, retired from the ring to become a promoter with a gym and a stable of well-trained fighters. He taught boxing as a science, encouraging combinations of blows, the parry, and the counterpunch. And he advocated the use of gloves.

Many amateur fighters trained at Gentleman Jack's gym. They carried his teaching methods throughout England and helped advocate boxing as an art to be mastered by anyone who wished to call himself a gentleman.

While members of the upper classes in Continental Europe continued to resort to swords whenever differences or points of honor became an issue, Englishmen began to put on the gloves. An affair of honor was no longer a life or death matter for the English gentleman, and this marked an important change in attitude.

It was a change that helped establish England as a sporting nation with an enthusiasm for all sports that con-

An early drawing of Chinese boxers suggests that kicking was a home-grown tactic and not something that developed out of Greek influence.

tinues to this day both on the home island and in the many areas of the world that England colonized.

When some of these distant colonies were established, however, Englishmen discovered that the natives had already invented their own style of boxing. In many Eastern countries, boxers could hit with their feet as well as their fists.

Kick boxing suggests the influence of Greek pankration, but it is more likely that the style had its roots in karate or kung fu, two ancient systems of self-defense.

Karate can trace its legendary beginnings to Zen priests who reportedly introduced it in China in 517 A.D. There, Buddhists became masters and added new techniques. As it spread throughout the East, karate took on different forms and styles. Generally, however, all styles combine kicks, blows with the open hand, throws, holds, body turns, crouches, leaps, and falls.

Although kung fu also had ancient beginnings, it probably was one of the first distinct styles to evolve from an early form of karate. Sometimes called Chinese boxing or Chinese karate, kung fu makes more use of the open hand and follows more stylized moves, many of which are modeled on animal motions or positions of attack.

Karate and kung fu today are further divided into different styles. Kung fu, for instance, has the so-called internal style, which emphasizes evasive action and use of an opponent's force against him, and the external style, which relies more on brute strength with blocks and strikes executed with force.

Like judo, karate and kung fu make it possible for a small man or woman to disable or at least discourage a large attacker. This has given these weaponless defensive sports world-wide popularity.

In the United States, according to a 1974 count, there were 164,800 schools offering classes in kung fu and karate. Although not a spectator sport on a level even approaching boxing, these eastern skills far outdrawn boxing in interest as participation sport among amateurs.

Chapter Five

Rome: Gladiators & Chariot Races

Etruscans, usually thought of as passive victims of an expanding Rome, had a dark and bloody facet to their culture.

It is best illustrated by wall paintings found in the tomb of Augers that dates back to pre-Roman times. The paintings show a deadly contest between a slave and a hunter.

The slave is armed with a club, but a hood is tied over his head so that he cannot see. The hunter, wearing a mask, has a tracking dog on a leash.

In one scene the slave is vainly trying to attack his pursuer. In another, the hound has downed the slave who is bleeding from several wounds while the hunter stands by with a noose ready to end the deadly game.

Archeologists believe that the paintings were made at a time when human sacrifice was part of the Etruscan religious ritual, a ritual that had become a game.

Other Etruscan tombs, dating back to about 600 B.C. reflect Greek influence. They include scenes of boxing, running, jumping, discus throwing, and chariot racing with no hint of blood.

But while Etruscans learned to appreciate pure athletics, they apparently retained an interest in sport as a spectacle with plenty of violence and blood. Certainly this interest influenced Roman culture. The tradition of the gladiator seems to have been fully established well before the Roman Empire came into being.

The last independent band of Etruscans had just been suppressed when, in 254 B.C., a funeral held for Brutus Pera featured gladiators fighting to the death in Rome's cattle forum. In 216 B.C. forty-four gladiators fought at the funeral of Marcus Lepidus, and when Titus Flaminius, the general who subdued Greece, died in 175 B.C., seventy-four gladiators fought for three days.

The only similarity between these festivals and those of the Greeks is that both can trace their beginnings to funeral rites.

Romans loved armed combat. Constant wars during Roman expansion did not provide enough of it. Combat had to be staged at every opportunity.

Gladiators trooped into the arenas on all major holidays as well as state funerals. And when a politician needed public support, he staged a special gladiator spectacle. News of victory by a distant army was good excuse for a lavish celebration that featured gladiators.

Watching gladiators became a Roman passion. By the beginning of the first century B.C. there were twenty-one gladiator arenas in Italy. A hundred years later, the number had grown to fifty, and when the second century A.D. began, there were sixty-four arenas.

Though badly weathered, a first century A.D. bas-relief clearly shows the grim intensity of the gladiator games. "Sudden death" was more than a figure of speech in Roman arenas.

Augustus Caesar, one of the few emperors who appreciated Greek athletic competition, tried to limit gladiator games to two a year with no more than 120 men taking part. He realized that political power was being gained by the wealthy through their ability to stage games and win public support.

Caesar, however, was unable to control privately financed games. They continued, and often two hundred, even three hundred men battled before the frenzied crowds. Augustus himself estimated that more than ten thousand gladiators had fought during his forty-one-year reign.

Wealthy men bought and trained gladiators just as

the wealthy of modern times buy and train race horses. Gladiators were slaves, and they were doomed. The strongest and the most skillful of them might survive many battles in the arena, but when age weakened them, they were sure to fall a younger man.

In the search for novelty, the games were often turned into circuses. The Emperor Titus who ruled from 79 to 81 A.D. managed to crowd ten thousand fighters into a single arena. The Emperor Domitian, however, won the prize for the unusual when he brought women and dwarfs into the arena.

Battles with hungry lions and tigers, introduced as a novelty, soon became common. While most Romans seemed to love any duel between man and beast, Cicero, the philosopher and orator who lived from 106 to 43 B.C., deplored the cruelty.

"What possible pleasure," he asked, "can any person of sensitivity gain from the spectacle of a weak human torn to pieces by a wild carnivore of far greater strength, or of a superb animal stabbed to death by a hunting spear?"

Influential as he was, however, Cicero failed to change public tastes in this matter.

Even the slave revolt that threw Rome into three years of turmoil brought only a temporary stay in the passion for gladiators.

The revolt was sparked by the gladiators. It began in 73 B.C. when two hundred of them kept by the wealthy Lantulus Batiates tried to escape. Seventy-eight succeeded and established a rebel camp on the slopes of Mount Vesuvius, where they promptly elected a leader. They made a wise choice in Spartacus.

He was a natural leader with military cunning. A Roman soldier, he had deserted, been captured, and then sold into slavery to be trained for the arena.

Soon after being chosen leader of the small band, Spartacus called upon all the slaves of Italy to revolt. People flocked to him by the thousands. Many had to be turned away because they were in no condition to fight, but many others joined the growing ranks.

Spartacus soon found himself at the head of sixty thousand men. He saw to it that they were well-armed and well-trained. And when the Roman legions marched to attack the camp, they were turned away in defeat.

Defeat of Rome's best soldiers at the hands of slaves shocked the empire, while the slaves themselves became more confident. More and more volunteers flocked to the rebel camp.

Spartacus devised a battle plan. He knew that slaves, no matter how well they fought in battle, would not be able to rule Rome. Free citizens would never submit to a government of former slaves. So the only sensible thing to do was to lead the army out of Italy. Beyond the outposts of empire, the slaves could find new lives as free men.

It was a noble plan, but it didn't work. The slaves wanted to destroy the legions and rob free citizens. Spartacus did manage to lead his men northward toward the Alps. And he did prevent a direct attack on Rome. But his men, eager for loot and revenge, grew unruly, and by laying waste to the countryside, they lost any sympathy that they might have gained from free men.

The army began to suffer its first defeats. Spartacus was turned away from the Alps and forced southward. He hoped now to lead his men out of Italy by boats to Sicily and on to Africa, but before he could carry out this plan, the army was badly beaten and its ranks divided.

Spartacus died in a fierce battle. Reports say that he was beaten to his knees with mortal wounds but fought on until his last breath, his body hacked beyond recognition.

A typical gladiator helmet gave full protection to the man's head, allowing him to fight on, even after he might be severely wounded on the body or limbs.

The remains of the army turned north, encountered Pompey's legions, and were overwhelmed. Those not killed in the fighting were crucified. Their bodies were left on crosses that lined the road to Rome as grisly warnings against further rebellion. Thus ended three years of chaos sparked by a band of gladiators.

The revolt did nothing to improve the lot of gladiators. They returned to the arenas to fight without pity. Heavily armed, they fought with swords, lances, barbed pikes and forks, and metal nets. When a man fell, his fate was often left to the crowd. They signaled thumbs up if they wanted him saved; thumbs down if he should die.

Experts in Roman history have long tried to explain the excesses in bloody entertainment. None of the explanations seem adequate.

Some historians say gladiator games filled a religious need. The festivals were a holy exercise, a form of worship. Others say they provided a sense of community and unified Romans both politically and spiritually. Still others say the games were a way of celebrating the remarkable economic and military successes that Romans were experiencing.

Romans themselves defended their love of gladiator games by saying that they were educational experiences. It improved the mind and the soul to see slaves and convicts die in the arena.

Clearly we lack full understanding of the Roman mind and soul. And ironically, while Romans were supporting lavish spectacles of death, they were also encouraging the continuation of athletic games in the Greek tradition. True, growing emphasis was put on boxing, pankration, and chariot racing, the events promising most action and violence, but running, jumping, javelin throwing, and other pure tests of skill and strength were not ignored.

Although they did not participate in them, Romans liked to watch the traditional games. The athletes who were not slaves were almost all professionals, and some of them won fame and wealth in their travels from one arena to the next.

The professional, no longer competing for the honor of his home state or town, now gave loyalty to his guild. One of these guilds, the Company of Hercules, had temples and treasuries in every Roman city and provided space in gymnasia where members could train.

Almost all members of the Company of Hercules, founded in the second century A.D., were Greeks, natives either of the mainland or of former Greek colonies.

The professionals, like today's pro athletes, were entertainers, and they tried to please the fans wherever they performed. Eventually, traditional games began to draw bigger crowds than gladiators.

Boxing attracted the most interest while chariot racing attracted the heaviest betting. And a race of several chariots, each pulled by a team of four horses, provided plenty of thrilling action.

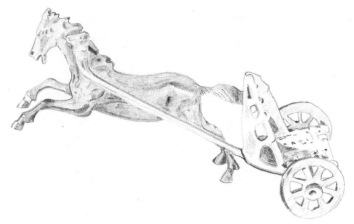

*One horse is missing in this small statue of a chariot. The
statue may have been a temple offering, but it was just as likely
a home decoration depicting the favorite sport of the day.*

Locked wheels, tangled harness, and jolting upsets
made it a dangerous sport. Success required skilled drivers
and well-trained teams.

As interest in gladiators waned, more and more of
Rome's rich transferred their investments from fighting
slaves to stables of horses. Chariot drivers became the high-
est paid athletes of their day. Although most of them began
their lives as slaves, they could expect to retire as million-
aires if they survived.

Any Roman could easily obtain a bank loan if he was
lucky enough to persuade a chariot driver to cosign the
note. Chariot driving in Roman times thus offered the
rags-to-riches opportunity that has become almost com-
monplace in professional sports today.

Because of rising costs, it soon became impossible for
one man to support a racing stable on his own. Investment
companies were thus formed to finance breeding and training of horses and development of drivers. Each company
was marked by distinctive colors. At first four companies
dominated. The Red, Blue, White, and Green teams were
easily identified by the colors of their harnesses, chariots,
and drivers' garb. Eventually, the red and white companies
faded under the dominance of the blue and green.

Fan devotion to one or the other of these teams outstripped political loyalties. Arguing the merits of the blue or green was a common pastime in Roman wineshops.

The major arena for chariots was the huge Circus Maximus located between Rome's Palatine and Aventine hills. It had seating for one hundred and eighty thousand spectators, a greater capacity than most modern stadia.

It enclosed an area 328 feet wide and 2,083 feet long, but in the Fourth Century A.D., its dimensions were expanded.

Most races were seven laps around a narrow oval, a distance of some five miles. The usual race meet lasted three days, with up to twenty-four races each day. Most programs alternated chariot races with horses races. Whole fortunes could change hands with a single race, and favorites were touted by soothsayers who made tidy profit from the fans.

Strangely, despite their fame, jockeys and charioteers never won the social status accorded free citizens. And it was considered demeaning for a citizen to participate. Thus, in the First Century A.D., when Nero took the reins of a chariot team, he made more enemies than friends. The race, of course, was fixed so he would win, but his victory did not bring the public support he anticipated.

In the Roman view, the only place of dignity in the arena was in the stands. This view was held steadfastly until the empire crumbled under the crush of Germanic tribes.

The centuries of change and confusion that followed the fall of Rome did not encourage sports. And when games did finally become popular once more, social attitudes had gone through profound change.

Chapter Six

Lance and Sword

On the surface the armed combat that emerged as a sport during the Dark Ages was not much different from gladiator battles. The contestants wore armor and attacked each other with swords and lances.

But the underlying differences were vast. The Roman fighters were slaves, performing to entertain. The fighters of the new era were nobles in the quest of fame, honor, and other virtues of the day. A new tradition called chivalry dominated society. Its roots were bedded in pagan beliefs that prospered well in a Christian climate.

The Goths, Saxons, Lombards, Franks, and other tribes that inherited the territories once ruled by Rome had long held their warriors in high respect. They were a class apart, and membership in the warrior class had to be earned. A candidate for membership had to prove both skill and bravery in battle or some other test of arms. Only then could he be considered for initiation in secret ceremonies. But there was one other requirement. Before he could become a knight the candidate had to prove that he was of noble blood.

Early Christianity, concerned with the expansion of faith, reinforced the fraternity of the warrior knights. It soon became their sworn duty to protect the faith and set a Christian example in thought and deed.

Further reinforcement for knighthood rose from the political realities of the day. Europe was split into hundreds of small realms. Many were controlled by belligerent rulers eager to expand their territory, many by tyrants who kept their peasants in virtual slavery.

A ruler needed a class of loyal warriors for both internal as well as external protection. From the beginning, knights filled this need perfectly. By definition, a knight was a man who served a higher master.

The word knight stems from the Old English *cniht,* which originally meant a foot soldier who was loyal to his master. When horses became almost the exclusive property of the nobility, the meaning of the word evolved to describe a mounted warrior.

Although the system of knighthood certainly had its faults, it did provide a vital measure of stability in an age noted for its unrest. And being a knight did wonderful things for one's physical fitness.

A knight was expected to be handy with battle-axe, lance, and sword. He had to be at home both in the saddle and in a suit of heavy armor. Constant training was necessary to perfect the fighting skills. It took hard, monotonous work to keep fit, but competition soon evolved to relieve the monotony.

The French are traditionally credited with inventing mock battles, but it is likely that knights in many regions had long been charging each other with blunted lances, making the armor clang with unedged swords, and thinking it good fun. The French, we can assume, were the first to turn this kind of fun into an event.

Simply hauling yourself into the saddle while wearing a coat of mail was a great achievement. A medieval drawing suggests that it took painful effort.

The field for a mock battle under the French system was fenced with wattles, woven sticks and poles to separate spectators from warriors. Armored knights armed with lances formed into two groups, one at each end of the field. Then on the signal of a trumpet, the two groups charged each other at full gallop. The idea was for each man to pick out an opponent as he charged and unseat him with his lance.

After this opening phase, those still in the saddle dismounted and everyone resumed fighting on foot with swords or battle-axes.

These *bouhourts,* as the French called them, soon became highly popular in other lands. They were well established in England by the twelfth century. One writer of the day, William FitzStephens, left a colorful description of bouhourts held near London.

"Every Sunday in Lent, after luncheon, a crowd of young gentlemen ride out into the fields on good war horses, all trained to maneuver and charge. Sons of the citizenry march out through the gates, equipped with spears and shields, the pikes of the younger men with forked points but with the iron head removed. They fight a mock battle and skirmish together like warriors. This exercise is attended by numerous courtiers when the king is in or near London, and scions of baronial and other important families who are under the age to be girded with arms resort there for these fights. Hope of victory inflames them all. Neighing, the chargers stamp and champ, finding waiting unendurable. At length to the trample of hooves the young riders divide into two groups. Some chase after others without catching them. Others unhorse their comrades and dash past."

Mock battles remained popular for many years, but they were eventually replaced entirely by individual combat. Watching just two men, either mounted or on foot, go at one another was much less confusing than the melee of mock battle. And individual combat rarely left any doubt about the winner.

Knights were proud of their ancestry and wore coats that colorfully displayed the family crest or symbol. The motif was repeated on the knight's shield and on banners carried by his pages. This system of symbols, known as heraldry, first appeared about 1150 A.D.

Refinements and complexities were added through the centuries. Each color had a special meaning, and special combinations of colors and symbols could be used to indicate rank as well as ancestry.

Many a knight also wore the token of the lady he held in esteem. Usually a glove or a scarf, the token did not necessarily denote romantic interest. The knight felt hon-

When the artist drew a jousting scene he rarely failed to show the ladies, and in this case the ladies seem more interested in their conversation than in the action in the lists.

ored when given a token, and wearing it was an act of respect.

The ladies themselves took special seats at the edge of the field where they could encourage their favorites with smiles or waves of a dainty hand.

Jousting, the mounted phase of battle, led in popularity among both spectators and participants. It was staged in a fenced area known as a list, and on some lists a low bisecting fence served to separate the charging horses and reduce risk of injury to them.

By tradition, the winner of any engagement captured the loser. To regain his freedom, the loser had to offer his horse and armor as ransom.

If the winner was a gentleman, however, he would refuse this offer and treat his captive to a banquet. And if the loser was a gentleman, he would then present the winner with a small gift. The winner, accepting this as ransom, released his man, and the two would part as friends.

But things did not always work this way. Some knights, as you might suspect, were not gentlemen. They made a business of their captures, demanding full ransom of armor, horse, and harness. This loot would either be sold to a broker or sold directly back to the original owner at a stiff price.

Most knights were outraged at this behavior. It was unthinkable that a man of noble birth could behave in such ungentlemanly fashion. The professional knight, however, did not mind offending his fellows. He traveled about from one list to the next, making sure to pick opponents less experienced and less skilled than he. He lost respect but gained a livelihood.

The only defense against the professional was to tighten up entry to the lists. Heralds, who set entry requirements, cut off the hand of anyone who entered the lists and was unable to prove his nobility.

At some tournaments, a knight not only had to recite his ancestry but also satisfy the heralds that his conduct had been above reproach. Some professional knights could thus be barred on charges of immoral or un-Christian behavior, but there was a problem. Under the code of chivalry, a knight could always erase past sins simply by repeating his vows to his heavenly god and earthly master.

The professional knight, however, was a small risk compared with the physical danger of the list. Though both horse and rider were protected by armor specially designed to deflect lances, fatal accidents were common.

With the riders charging at full gallop, the impact of the lances, even blunted ones, was tremendous. A well-placed lance could lift a man from his saddle, armor and all, and send him flying to a bone-crunching impact with the ground. If the man could hold his seat, there was a chance that the lance might shatter in a shower of danger-ous splinters.

Knights who could split a dozen lances between them without a fall earned the respected title of "forest sweep-ers" because of the timber they destroyed. But a shattered lance was a lethal weapon.

Montagu, first earl of Salisbury, was killed in the lists at Windsor, and his grandson, Sir William Montagu, was killed in the same place while jousting against his father.

At a Saxony tournament in 1177, sixteen knights were killed in a single day. Sixty knights reportedly died on the lists at Neuss in the year 1251.

Pope Innocent II tried to put a stop to jousting in 1139 when he denied Christian burial for anyone killed at the sport. The knights all but ignored the edict, but they remained devout as ever, usually having a mass said just before taking the saddle.

In the minds of the nobles, jousting had become more than a test of strength and skill. It was a test of Christian faith and piety. At times, it even settled arguments and disputes of honor. The just cause was the winning cause.

So jousting continued as a popular sport long after the heavily armored horsemen had been replaced by light cavalry on the battlefield. A jousting tournament was an important political and social affair, a gathering of the ruling class.

Good manners were the rule. A knight of low rank was expected to lose to his betters. But accidents still hap-pened.

In celebration of the peace of Cateau-Cambrésis, King Henry II of France called his nobles to a tournament at Paris. It was held on June 30, 1559, and it began in a happy spirit.

The people cheered their king as he rode out in full armor to face Gabriel, Count of Montgomery. The count's lance had been weakened so it would splinter on the king's armor with no danger of unseating him.

When the two met, the lance broke as expected, but the count did not lift the splintered stump quickly enough. It found a crack in the king's helmet and pierced his temple. The king died soon after being carried from the field.

The tragedy sent waves of shock through all of Europe. Enthusiasm for the sport of jousting died with the king.

Although jousting is no more, other traditions of chivalry live on. Tipping one's hat to a lady goes back to the days when a knight raised the visor of his helmet so that friends could recognize him. Symbols of heraldry still appear on business letterheads and advertisements.

In sports, modern fencing can trace its roots back to the knights and their war games. Skill with swords was considered necessary for all European gentlemen long after jousting died out. And the sword was the gentleman's weapon in affairs of honor. Duels with swords were common up until the end of the last century.

Of course, if a man had to defend his honor with a sword, he had to be taught the fundamentals and he had to practice. Fencing was thus part of the gentleman's education, and teaching the art was a noble profession. Many masters had their own schools and gymnasiums where pupils could practice daily.

Instruction usually began with the foil, a light weapon with a very thin blade. When the basic thrusts, parries, and steps were mastered, the student could then advance to the épée, which called for quick and accurate thrusts, or the saber which combined thrusting and slashing and emphasized defense of the entire body.

Under the code of the duel, the first wound usually settled differences. Rarely would gentlemen battle to the death.

The duels for sport, however, held in the gymnasiums or sword clubs might continue until a deep wound needed attention.

Just a few generations ago, the scar from such a wound was a much desired decoration among the young men of Germany. It was a macho symbol, one that recalled the bygone days when knighthood still flowered in the Old World.

Chapter Seven

Ritual of the Ring

The bull, most dangerous of all animals, has been feared and worshipped since the beginning of civilization.

Today when a Spanish bullfighter, armed only with a cape and short sword, stands before a charging bull a very ancient ritual is being reenacted.

The rules of this ritual are precise. The man must master the beast without show of fear. He must work the animal with his cape, invite it to charge again and again. Although the tips of the animal's lethal horns may pass within a fraction of an inch of the man's body, he must not jump aside or flinch.

Finally, when the charges or passes have slowed and the bull's head is low with fatigue, the man must thrust his sword between the passing animal's shoulder blades at an exact downward angle to cut the aorta.

The vital target is small, no more than a few inches round, and the thrust must be timed to the split second. But if done properly, the bull will drop in its tracks, dead.

Most North Americans are horrified by bullfighting, looking on it not as a sport but as an exercise in cruelty. A

Spanish or a South American bullfighting fan, however, will be quick to tell you that bullfighting is no more cruel than hunting. In fact the bull has a fighting chance not given the hunter's quarry. And for the devotee of the ring, a bullfight is more than a sport. It is the struggle of good over evil, or light over darkness.

It is said that the spectator at a bullfight loses all his hate, jealousy, and other evil emotions. Evil dies with the bull. Sociologists believe that if bullfighting in Spain should cease, the crime rate in that country would soar, and that the famous courtliness and good manners of Spanish gentlemen and women would be no more.

The origins of modern day bullfighting are clouded in the past, but study of what we do know, both from the historical record and from mythology and legend may help us understand and perhaps even appreciate the ritual of the ring.

Far to the east in the Indus Valley of present day Pakistan, where a civilization flourished in 1500 B.C., archeologists have found clay seals decorated with scenes of bulls and athletes.

On some seals, an athlete is shown wrestling a bull to the ground by its horns. On others, athletes appear to be vaulting over a charging bull. Cave paintings in Africa suggest that bull vaulting was also practiced there at a very early time.

On Crete, bull vaulting and bull worship date back to the beginnings of the Minoan civilization. In fact, so many vase and wall paintings depicting bull vaulting have been found there that we can study methods and style in some detail.

Perhaps the most striking thing about these paintings is the size of the bulls. Compared with the figures of the acrobats, the animals always seem of heroic size. It may be

A Cretan wall painting shows the disproportionate size of the bulls that has long puzzled scholars. Were the acrobats children? We can't be sure.

only artistic exaggeration, but perhaps boys and girls, light and not fully grown, were the only athletes allowed to participate, and the bulls look bigger than life by comparison.

The vaulter first had to stand fearlessly before the charging bull. Then at just the right moment the vaulter jumped toward the animal, grabbing a horn in each hand. The bull, feeling the weight, tossed its head instinctively, thus launching the acrobat over its back. A good vaulter made at least one full turn before landing on his or her feet in the wake of the bull.

Obviously, a mistake could be fatal. Mistakes were certainly made. Some of the Cretan paintings show young athletes being gored by angry bulls.

Experts on modern bullfighting say that a full-grown man could not vault over a bull in the Cretan manner. Did the ancient artists invent all these scenes? Was what seemed a popular sport nothing but an imaginary activity?

We almost have to conclude that bull vaulting was practiced through many centuries, but because of the relative scale between beast and vaulters it has been suggested that highly trained acrobats were selected for their light builds. Some indeed may have been children.

Mythology has no lack of tales about fierce bulls and the heroes who faced and conquered them. Symbolically, these tales represent victory of courage or good over fear or evil.

One story was part of the early Persian's religious faith. Mithra, the Persian god of light and good, was at first a minor divinity, but then, according to the myth, he captured a wild bull.

It was a huge animal, but Mithra overcame his fear and killed it on an altar of sacrifice. The beast's blood flowed into the sand and nourished it. Beneficial crops sprang up, and from the bull's body came all other things useful to man.

To the Persians, Mithra's victory over the bull marked the beginning of the good life. And Mithra was worshipped thereafter as the most important of all gods.

The story of Mithra became the foundation for a cult among Greeks and later among Romans. Rites of Mithraism included secret meetings, feasting, fasting, and baptism.

By the Second Century A.D., Mithraism had become the most important single cult in the Roman Empire. It was particularly popular among Roman soldiers. Mithra, to them, was the ideal fighting man, a symbol of bravery, a benefactor, and a companion.

A common art motif in carvings and paintings throughout the empire depicted Mithra slaying the bull. The scene is remarkably similar to the technique of modern bullfighting, but strangely very few carvings of the god and the bull have been found in Spain, where bullfighting was to become a modern sport.

The transition from Mithraism to Christianity did not require a revolution in faith. The central theme of Christianity also dealt with the conflict between good and evil, and followers of Mithraism were already familiar with baptism and other rites shared by the two faiths.

Greek mythology has bulls by the herd. Zeus once adopted the guise of a bull to abduct Europa, the beautiful daughter of the King of Phoenicia. Europa was tending her father's cattle when the bull appeared among the cows. As soon as the god in bull form persuaded her to sit upon his back, he charged off into the sea and carried her to Crete.

There Zeus assumed his own form and lived with Europa for several years. She bore three sons, the eldest of whom was Minos who long ruled as king of Crete. Some of his heirs, it appears, bore the same name.

Minos kept a huge wild bull, a symbol of his divine heritage that was undoubtedly honored with sacrifice and worship.

One of the labors of Hercules was to go to Crete, capture the bull of Minos and bring it back to the Peloponnesus. The benefit of this feat has to be questioned, for Hercules turned the huge beast loose, and the animal began at once to terrorize the countryside.

Minos, or one of his heirs by the same name, had a wife called Pasiphäe who bore a strong and handsome son called Androgeos or Earthman. But Pasiphäe, after an unnatural mating with a sacred bull, also gave birth to a monster, the bull-headed Minotaur.

Having an appetite for human flesh, the Minotaur was hidden in a labyrinth beneath Minos' palace.

While the monster was locked up in the dark passages of the labyrinth, Androgeos travelled to Greece where he became very popular because of his good looks and his skill and strength as a wrestler.

Growing jealous over the young man's success, a local

ruler arranged to match Androgeos against the bull that had been destroying crops and killing peasants. The prince bravely accepted the challenge, but the bull killed him.

Suspecting treachery, Minos sent his fleet to the mainland and defeated the Greeks. In the terms of surrender, Minos demanded that every ninth year the Greeks send seven boys and seven girls to Crete to be offered to the Minotaur.

The Greeks stuck to the agreement until the heroic Theseus came to the rescue. First Theseus captured the bull that had been terrorizing the countryside. After sacrificing it to the gods, he sailed to Crete to take on the Minotaur.

Androgeos' sister, Ariadne, secretly helped Theseus by giving him a thread to unwind as he searched the labyrinth. After killing the monster, Theseus found his way out by following the thread.

Theseus' feat freed the Greeks from the cruel pact. It marked, according to the legend, the rise of Greek influence over the Mediterranean world, and the loss of power for Crete.

Bull sports continued in other places after Crete's decline. In northern Greece young horsemen enjoyed a sport little different from bulldogging in today's rodeos. The rider, while running his steed beside the bull, would leap to the bull's back and then grab and twist its horns to wrestle it to the ground.

Greek horsemen demonstrated the sport in Rome, but there is no evidence that it ever became popular among the Romans or helped inspire the eventual development of modern bullfighting.

It was the invasion from Africa by the Moors in the eighth century B.C. that introduced a form of bullfighting in Spain. Mounted Moors had long fought bulls with lances. We do not know the origin of this African sport. It had little relation to the bull-leaping of Crete and only slight similarity to the bulldogging practiced by Greek horsemen.

The Moors prodded the bull with their sharp lances while doing their best to keep their horses clear of the angry animal's charges and thrusts. Risk was greater for the horse than rider, but the sport just the same was a test of courage as well as horsemanship.

The Moors' game can still be recognized as the first phase of a modern bullfight when mounted lancers, called picadors, enter the ring. The picadors' purpose is to wound the bull in the neck just enough to weaken its powerful thrusting muscles. The wounds make the bull slightly less dangerous and much angrier than before.

In the early days of Spanish bullfighting, a picador's horse was unprotected and frequently gored. Old nags ready for the glue factory were commonly used for the dangerous work. Today, a picador rides a horse that is draped in heavy padding that reduces the risk. Just the same, a bull can sometimes upset both horse and rider.

When a rider is thrown, men with capes run quickly into the ring to distract the bull from the fallen man and give him time to remount.

After the picadors have finished their work, they are replaced by the banderilleros for the second phase of the performance. It is their job to stick barbed darts, called banderillas, in the bull's neck.

The job is not easy. A banderillero is on foot and the only way he can reach the bull is by tempting it to charge him. Then, in a well-timed move, he must plant his darts and step clear of the horns as the animal dashes by.

A graceful performance and a well placed dart brings thundering cheers from the crowd, but clumsiness, any show of fear, or a dart that fails to stick prompts whistles and boos.

When the darts, brightly festooned with paper, have been used up, the banderilleros leave the ring to the matador, the star performer of the entertainment. He enters alone with a cape and short sword to begin the final phase.

Theoretically, the bull's neck wounds prevent him from lifting his head. But the matador must watch the animal closely to detect any special moves or strengths that the bull may have retained. The bull may habitually hook to one side with its horns, and this would warn the matador to have the bull pass with that side away from him.

The passes are controlled entirely with the cape. Although it is traditionally made of red cloth, it is motion not color that attracts the bull. Instinctively charging at

Controlling a bull with nothing but a cape is a feat of skill and daring unmatched in any other sport, but because the bull must die, it is not likely that bullfighting's popularity will grow.

anything that moves, he will drive his horns at the cape again and again.

The matador must not move. A backward jump not only risks a goring from the bull, but it also invites boos and whistles from the fans who interpret it as a loss of form and courage.

When a pass is complete, the matador may then move to face the bull once more and present the cape for another charge. Skillful capework creates a ballet of man and beast in life and death drama.

The tension is broken at the end of each pass only by the chorus of *Olé!* It is the crowd's traditional cheer of appreciation for skill and courage.

Eventually, after the bull tires and his charges become slower and less ferocious, the matador readies his sword behind the cape. When the beast charges yet again, the sword is brought up over the cape. Just as the bull begins the pass, the matador thrusts the sword down between the animal's shoulder blades. If the point is properly placed and the blade is at the proper angle, the sword will plunge through the vital aorta, killing the bull instantly while the crowd roars its approval.

But bullfights do not always end this way. If the sword is just a few inches off target, the bull will not fall. Another matador will have to be called in to do the job properly, while the first man, if he has escaped goring, must leave the ring in disgrace.

Few of the famous matadors have lived to retirement age. Bulls learn quickly, and will take advantage of any errors the man might make in the ring. One rare veteran who hung up his cape after twenty-one years in the ring, was gored an average of three times a season during his career. It is a remarkable testimony to human courage that a man would return to the ring after just one goring. But most matadors do come back again and again until they are fatally gored. Bullfighting fans demand a great deal from their heroes.

It is not clear exactly how bull lancing of the Moors evolved into today's three-phase sport. We do know that the Christian knights who finally drove the Moors out of Spain in the thirteenth century, adopted bull lancing. In fact, there was a lively rivalry between Moor and Christian in the sport.

Spanish knights established lancing as a pastime for the aristocratic or horse-owning class, and for many years, every celebration of the Spanish court included bull lancing. It thus became associated with holidays and festivals.

By the eighteenth century, however, the aristocracy began to lose interest in the sport. Noblemen began to let their footmen represent them in the ring. This step introduced the unmounted bullfighter, and the unmounted phases of the sport were apparently influenced by the need to subdue the beast gradually. A man simply could not work a bull safely with a cape until after its neck muscles had been weakened with barbed darts.

Soon a professional class of bullfighters took charge of the sport and established a star system that pitted the best men against the best bulls. The ritual of killing the bull with the short sword thrust between the shoulder blades was probably adopted because it simply proved to be the quickest, most humane way to make the kill.

But isn't it remarkable that countless carvings of the god Mithra show him killing a bull in the same way? Other traces of Mithraism are easily found in the modern ring. For instance, the colorful clothing worn by the men is called the dress of lights, recalling the pagan theme of light over dark.

Fans idolize the great matadors because, like Mithra,

the matadors have mastered fear to destroy a great beast.

No matter what your opinion of bullfighting might be, you have to agree that it recalls very ancient religious ideas, and these ideas remain important to a civilized people who have made no small contribution to the civilized world.

Chapter Eight

Flight of Arrows

Invention of the bow and arrow, along with control of fire, development of language, and discovery of the wheel ranks among the most important achievements of man.

It happened at least fifty thousand years ago, perhaps even one hundred thousand years ago, and no one can guess where or how the first bow was made. By the time recorded history began, distribution of the bow was worldwide.

True, some primitive tribes never developed the strong bows that were so effective as weapons of war, but this cannot be taken as a sign of backwardness.

In thick jungle growth where the native hunter stalked small game, a long shot was not needed. That the native could make good use of a weak weapon is actually a testimony of resourcefulness. With points dipped in natural poisons that stunned or killed, the small arrow could bring down large game and even a human enemy when necessary.

Some archeologists believe that the bow and arrow may have evolved from a simple sling used to give a lance greater velocity. Others hold the more romantic notion that the weapon evolved from a musical instrument, a twine stretched on a bent stick.

The bow harp is still played by some primitive people. With an end of the bow held in the mouth, the string is plucked by one hand while the other grips the twine against the stick. Changes in tension of the grip changes the pitch.

Although we can't say how the bow and arrow evolved, we can say that it appeared with infinite variety both in design, materials used, and strengths.

The Egyptians developed a very powerful bow more than three thousand years ago. An inscription at Gizeh left by Amenhotep II who reigned from 1447 to 1420 B.C. declared that he shot an arrow through an inch-thick slab of copper and the arrow sailed on to strike a post some thirty feet beyond.

The bow and arrow was used to hunt game along the Nile and as a weapon in war. Just the same, archery did not appear to rank highly as a desired skill.

When bows and arrows appear among the furnishing of Egyptian burials, they rarely have the place of importance given household utensils or farm implements.

It may be that archery was a skill borrowed from neighboring tribes. Some inscriptions speak of bordering tribes as the "bow people." Possibly the bowmen who marched with Egypt's armies were imported mercenaries, foreigners who gave archery an alien character.

The people of Crete, noted for their seamanship and commerce, were also great archers. We know that Cretan bowmen did hire out as mercenaries to Egypt and other powers. The long-range, accurate shooting of Cretan archers gave advantage to any army that could afford their services.

With their wide travels, the Cretans spread the art of

bowmanship throughout the eastern Mediterranean. The Greeks took to the bow with enthusiasm.

Greek mythology teems with heroic archers. Apollo, the god of light, was credited in the Greek religion with inventing the bow. Poseidon's son, Orion, was a great hunter with the bow and arrow who traveled throughout the Greek world teaching his skill to mortals.

The bow was Hercules' favorite weapon, and it was used with deadly effect after he dipped his arrows in poison. Hercules' poison arrows were said to have given the Greeks the advantage in the Trojan war. It was the Greek hero Achilles, however, who died of a poisoned Trojan arrow.

The centaur Chiron, half man and half horse, was a master hunter with the bow, and at his death took his place in the heavens as the constellation Sagittarius.

Orion, after a troubled life on earth, also became a constellation.

The Greeks believed that Poseidon had given Orion the power to walk on water so that he could travel to all the Aegean islands and rid them of wild beasts. During his stay on the island of Chios, he fell in love with the king's daughter, Merope.

But the king, not wanting a wandering hunter in the family, blinded Orion and turned him out of the palace. Hephaestus, the god of fire, took pity on Orion and led him to the kingdom of the sun where his sight was restored.

With the huntress Artemis, Orion then spent many happy days tracking game. But he seemed to inspire jealousy. Orion's days were numbered.

Apollo, Artemis' brother and an excellent archer, decided that Orion and his sister were spending too much time together. Waiting until Orion had walked far out to sea by himself, Apollo suggested that Artemis test her

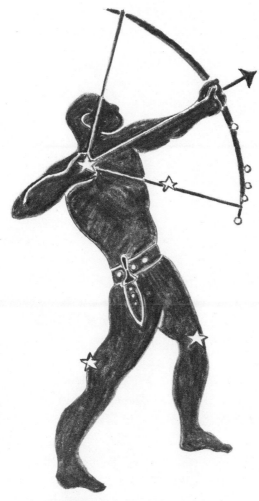

The star pattern of Orion does indeed
suggest an archer with a bright belt
and dagger. Take a look yourself
some winter night.

marksmanship. He pointed to a dot on the horizon and wagered that Artemis could not hit it.

Not suspecting that the dot was her hunting companion, Artemis confidently launched an arrow at the target, and of course, it struck and killed Orion.

Artemis remained innocent of the cruel plot until waves washed Orion ashore. Then, with flowing tears and loud cries of lament, she placed him in the skies where he shines to this day as one of the brightest constellations.

The Greeks were the first to make long bows of yew wood. The Greek word *toxon* meant both yew and bow. A yew bow was strong and it took a mighty arm to draw it. Even stringing it required great strength.

When Odysseus returned home disguised as a beggar after his long travels from Troy, his bow served to reveal his identity. Homer tells us that freeloading suitors who had been seeking the hand and wealth of Odysseus' wife, Penelope, had all tried and failed to string the bow. Only the beggar could perform the feat.

The suitors realized too late that Odysseus stood before them in beggar's disguise. He fired his arrows one after the other until all the suitors lay dead.

In light of the importance of the bow and arrow in both hunting and war, it is hard to understand why archery never became a sport to the Greeks. Youths certainly practiced to perfect their skill, but little mention is made of competition.

One inscription, however, has been found in the ruins of the Greek colony near the mouth of the River Bug in southern Russia. The ancient writing says that Anaxagoras, son of Demagoras, won a match by shooting an arrow 282 arogyias. An arogyia was about six feet, which would mean that Anaxagoras shot an arrow some 564 yards, a remarkable distance.

Scholars believe that such a distance could only have been achieved with a composite bow, a type that originated in the east. Unlike the long bow, which was carved from a single piece of wood, the composite bow was made up of layers of tough material bound and glued together.

By using thin layers of rigid wood, horn, sinew, or rawhide the composite bow did not rely on length for its power. Some bows were little more than four feet long. This compact design was well adapted for mounted archers.

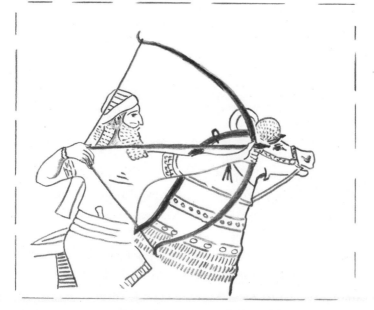

The composite bow shown in an Assyrian carving shows how the compact design made it ideal for the mounted archer. Notice unusual ear guards on the horse.

Invention of the composite bow has been credited to the Scythians, a wandering people who lived north of the Greeks and Persians about twenty-five hundred years ago. The Persians, and later the Turks, improved upon the bow for hunting and for war. And among the Turks, at least, archery became an important sport. Even after the bow was outlawed as a military weapon in 1591, Turkish archery continued to flourish.

Nearly every village in Turkey had a company of archers and a shooting ground for practice and competition. Competition was open to all. Peasants vied with Sultans to see who could shoot an arrow farthest.

Democratic as the sport might have been, the sultans got most of the publicity for their feats.

It was recorded that Murat IV, who reigned from 1623 to 1640, shot an arrow 796 yards. The Ottoman sultan, Mahmut II, shot an arrow 1,012 yards in 1831, and raised a monument to immortalize the achievement.

The bows that could shoot such distances were so stiff that they had to be drawn with the legs. The archer lay on his back with his hands on the string and his feet pressed on the bow. With a mighty effort, he straightened his legs and let the arrow fly. Archers trained with a routine of muscle-building exercises, but they also kept a close eye on the weather. The greatest distances were achieved when shooting with a strong wind.

For the Chinese, bowmanship was a mark of culture, and practice with the bow and arrow was a favorite pastime among the aristocracy. Although competition was popular, there is little mention of it in literature. This lack of mention can be explained by the Chinese gentleman's cultivated modesty. It was simply bad manners to boast of beating a rival at anything.

According to Chinese legend, the emperor Huang-ti invented the bow and arrow about 2000 B.C. It is more likely, however, that the weapon was introduced by those nomadic tribes on the western borders who repeatedly raided Chinese territory.

No matter what its origin, archery was taught to every young man. It was long a Chinese custom when a boy was born to a family to announce the event by hanging a bow and six arrows by the front door.

The Japanese developed a long bow that they could shoot with great force and accuracy. Although Japan's history is marked by centuries of isolation, it is remarkable that the marvelous Japanese bow was not copied by other peoples.

In islands of the South Pacific, bows and arrows were linked with magic. Polynesians believed it was tabu to use the bow in war. It could be shot in play only. The Polynesians competed for distance in marathon shooting matches. These events sometimes lasted for days. They began with offerings of meat and fruit to the gods and they ended with the losing team entertaining the winners with a big banquet. At no time were fires allowed. A fire on the shooting ground would bring bad luck to all.

Although their hibiscus wood did not make the strongest of bows, Polynesian archers could sometimes send an arrow 250 yards, a respectable distance.

Bushmen of South Africa had a special use for a special bow and arrow. When a young man wanted to propose to a girl he made a small bow of antelope horn and a tiny arrow. He then shot the arrow at the girl. If she threw it away, it meant that she was rejecting him, but if she kept the arrow she was saying "yes."

The native North Americans were skillful archers, and some developed bows that compared well with any in the Old World. Saxton Pope, who tested many native bows and put his findings in *Hunting with a Bow and Arrow*, achieved a shot of 256 yards with an English long bow. With a bow of the Yaki tribe, Pope sent an arrow 210 yards. He also had shots of more than 200 yards with Yana and Eskimo bows. The weakest bows were those of the Mojave, 110 yards, and the Osage, ninety-two yards, but even these bows were adequate for the native hunters.

Pope also did penetration tests on beef carcasses and found that the obsidian-tipped, Indian arrow went a surprising twenty-five percent deeper than modern, steel-tipped arrows.

Native American hunters had many target games with arrows and loved to compete and display their skills. Natives of the Mandan tribe apparently led all others in the rapid fire category. A Mandan brave could put eight arrows in flight before the first touched the ground. After many days of practice, Pope was able to put seven arrows in the air at one time.

For the greatest feats of bowmanship, however, we must look back to the yeomen of Old England. The word derives from *yew-men*, archers who used long bows made of yew.

It is not clear exactly how the long bow originated in England. Some accounts say it was a Welsh invention. Others say it had Norse origins and was brought to England by William the Conqueror. We do know that the bow became a formidable weapon for the English hunter and the soldier.

Although Robin Hood is a legendary character, many significant facts of history can be found in the stories about him. There were indeed outlaws who earned their livelihood through their bowmanship. They lived by poaching, and because killing the king's deer was a capital crime, they formed bands for mutual protection. In the thick forests some of these bands eluded the sheriff and his men for many years, and the outlaws undoubtedly had the sympathy of all peasants who struggled against authority. It is easy to understand how Robin Hood and his merry men became heroes of English folklore.

Bowmanship was encouraged in England with competitions and prizes. In times of peace there was no large army, but whenever England went to war, she could call on the citizen bowmen to fill the ranks and serve with credit.

In English military strategy, the long bow was a defensive weapon. Yeomen grouped on a hill could pour a torrent of deadly arrows on a charging enemy and cause havoc. The system worked again and again, and the French, a traditional enemy, never profited from the experience of losing to English yeomen.

Although they often outnumbered the English forces, French armies were soundly defeated at Cercy in 1346, at

Target practice with the long bow kept English marksmanship sharp. Competing for prizes was a common pastime open to all.

Poitiers in 1356, and at Agincourt in 1415. The French defeats can be blamed on entrenched social attitudes.

Clinging to the old ideas of chivalry, the French believed that war and skill at arms were the exclusive business of nobility. Peasants should not be encouraged to use weapons. At times it could even be dangerous to put weapons in the hands of unruly peasants. They might take it in their heads to revolt.

The French also believed that a mounted knight, encumbered with armor and slow as he might be, was the most formidable unit of the army.

English nobles also donned armor and rode to war, but they brought yeomen with them and stationed them in strategic positions of defense. The French had foot soldiers who were armed with crossbows. A bolt from a crossbow could pierce armor at close range, but because it had to be cocked with a lever it was not a rapid fire weapon. It was no match for the longbow.

It can be said that England's victories over the French were won on the archery ranges in Sunday afternoon competitions. English royalty put so much importance on archery that other sports were often discouraged.

When the Scottish game of golf threatened to become popular, it was banned by royal decree. After all, what use was a nine iron on the battlefield?

Of course, gunpowder eventually put the bow into retirement as a weapon of war, but the sport of archery never really died out in England. In 1660, Parliament, for the first time in centuries, omitted the bow in its list of weapons required by the army, but just thirteen years later, the annual archery contest at Scorton in Yorkshire was established. Now held at Oxford, the event is the oldest in the history of the sport.

Other meets, modeled after Scorton, were soon being held all over England. In 1795, the Turkish ambassador, attending one of these meets, was startled to see that the targets had been placed only 200 yards from the archers. The ambassador just happened to have a Turkish archer with him who demonstrated the power of the composite bow by shooting an arrow 482 yards.

The feat amazed the English archers, many of whom began making and using composite bows of their own design.

In America, archery as a sport rose from odd circumstances. As an Indian weapon, the bow and arrow was held in contempt by white settlers. The gun, after all, had defeated the bow and arrow and driven the Indians into submission. The bow was looked upon as an inferior weapon.

This attitude continued until after the Civil War. Then, with the Confederacy beaten and guns banned for a time in the South, two brothers, Maurice and Will Thompson, found good use for the bow.

When they returned to Georgia after the fighting, food and jobs were scarce. Farms had been plundered, and the Thompson home was in ruins. Most of their friends were without hope.

But when they had been boys, the brothers had made friends with a hermit who had taught them how to make and use bows and arrows. They decided to take to the woods and see if they could survive by hunting game.

They moved to the Everglades of Florida, where they set up a camp and made their own bows and arrows. Game was plentiful, and their woodland life turned into a happy adventure. They stayed in the woods several months, returning to civilization only after economic conditions had improved enough in the South for them to find work.

One brother eventually became a lawyer, the other an engineer, but they never forgot their experience in the woods. Maurice Thompson finally began writing magazine articles about it. The articles, which attracted wide attention, were collected and published in *The Witchery of Archery* in 1878.

The book enjoyed great popularity and almost overnight prompted formation of many archery clubs across the United States. In 1879, the clubs were affiliated under the National Archery Association, which has been active ever since.

Today there are more archers in the world than any time in history. It seems that Orion the Hunter has plenty of company.

Chapter Nine

Joys of Winter

Skiing as a sport, according to an old Norse legend, can be traced back to an unhappy marriage.

It is hard to say what Skada, the goddess of the snowy mountains, and Njord, the god of the seashore, saw in each other in the first place. But logic and love have always been strangers.

After Skada and Njord were married, Njord took her to his palace at the edge of the sea. As soon as she left her beloved mountains, however, Skada realized that the marriage was a mistake.

She tried to be a dutiful wife, but she was so homesick for the snowy slopes that she soon began to waste away. She pleaded with Njord to let her go back to the mountains. At first he refused, but at last he could no longer ignore Skada's unhappiness.

"Go," he said, "You're free to do whatever you wish."

Skada hastened back to her mountain home where she gathered up her bow and her arrows and tied on her skis. In no time at all she was schussing down the slopes, a free spirit off on the hunt.

After her long absence from the snow, Skada discovered that it was the pure joy of skiing that she had missed the most. Hunting was not as important. She went out to ski.

From time to time she went to the coast to visit Njord. He was always glad to see her, but he, too, had to admit the marriage was a mistake. He had married a ski bum.

Skiing as a sport is actually quite recent. For the people of the northern lands, skis were necessary for winter travel. Hunters needed them to track game. Herdsmen needed them to follow their animals.

The oldest ski ever found was dug from a bog near Hoting in the center of Sweden. It is believed to be at least four thousand years old. It, and others that are almost as old, do not look much like a modern ski. They are paddle-shaped and probably were used as a snowshoe when climbing and a runner when descending slopes.

Historians are convinced that the invention of skis

A Norse rock carving, at least four thousand years old, shows an unusually long pair of skis worn by what probably is supposed to be a hunter. The rabbit ears at least suggest a mask for stalking game.

occurred much more than four thousand years ago. Rock carvings and paintings, though difficult to date, suggest that skis were used in the Stone Age. One carving discovered in Norway shows two hunters wearing unusually long skis. If the proportions are correct, the skis would be about four yards long, quite different from the earliest specimens that have been found.

Other primitive pictures show men with skis of different lengths, a long ski that served as a runner, and a short ski that was used to push. The skier apparently traveled across the snow with scooter-like action.

The first written report on skiing appears in the works of Procopius, a sixth century A.D. Byzantine historian whose travels took him as far north as present-day Finland. There he saw Lapps using snow runners to follow their herds of reindeer.

The Italian artist who made this woodcut probably had never seen a person skiing. Certainly the runners shown here look impractical, if not impossible.

Procopius's report did not inspire his readers to take up skiing, nor did the Vikings do much to promote skiing on their far-ranging ventures of raiding, trading, and colonization. The Norsemen carried planklike skis with them, but because most of their trips were made in the summer season, there was little opportunity for skiing.

In their own land, however, skis played important roles in Norse history.

Late in the twelfth century when King Sverre of Norway was trying to put down revolt, his forces came under heavy attack at Oslo. Fearing for the safety of his grandson Haakon, the heir to the throne, the king picked two of the fastest skiers to carry the lad to safety on the far side of the Dovre Mountains.

Haakon III survived to rule a united Norway and is remembered today as one of his country's greatest rulers. His flight to safety is commemorated each year by a forty-mile, cross-country ski race along the same route his rescuers carried him.

In Sweden, the Vasaloppet race, a fifty-three-mile run from Mora to Sälen, marks another famous event in history with more than ten thousand skiers following a route once taken by the hero king, Gustavus Vasa.

In 1521, with much of Sweden under Danish rule, Vasa was trying to marshal an army to drive out the occupation forces. The men of the Dalarna district at first refused to answer Vasa's call to arms.

Discouraged, Vasa took to his skis and left the district, but soon after his departure, the men had a change of heart. They sent their fastest skiers after the king. They caught up with him after a wild dash across the mountains, brought him back, and with the aid of the Dalarnans, Vasa drove the Danes out of his country.

A pair of skis gave the Norse soldier an obvious advantage, and skiing was long part of military training. But it appears to have been optional until the 1720s when records reveal that all Norwegian soldiers were required to have skis and know how to use them. Training soon led to competition with soldiers vying for top speed on slalom courses that used rocks and trees for gate markers. There was also jumping competition, which began with runs off the sloping roofs of snow-covered buildings.

The sport of skiing, however, did not receive its first real boost until Scandinavians began to migrate and settle in other lands. The most receptive center for these ambassadors of skiing was the European Alps.

Although some peasants of Austria and Germany thought a man could sail over the snow only with the help of witchcraft, the more sophisticated people of these countries quickly adopted Norse skis and methods.

But there was a problem. The Alpine slopes were much steeper than those found in the rolling hills of Scandinavia. The safest way to come down a steep slope on skis calls for a switch-back descent with turns of at least ninety degrees. But the length and loose bindings of the Scandinavian skis made such turns next to impossible.

The only other choice was a schuss and a prayer straight down the hill. Early Alpine skiers had to be daredevils, and there were not enough daredevils around to give the sport much status.

Meanwhile, private citizens in Norway began to take interest in the military skiing competitions. By the time of the first national military races in 1767 at Christiania, now Oslo, private competitions were common.

Most of these early events were sprints over short courses. They tested speed more than endurance, but as interest grew so did the length of the races.

Although the town of Tromsö claims to have introduced the first cross-country race in 1843, it is likely that long endurance races were already common in the informal competitions of the day.

Meanwhile a farmer-skier near Christiania began experimenting with bindings. Sondre Nordheim, wanting more control for turning and stopping, fashioned stiff bindings made of birch roots. They held the boot firmly to the runner so that any foot movement was transferred instantly to the skis.

In the Alps, Nordheim's bindings, combined with stiffer, shorter skis, reduced the suicide element of the sport. Alpine skiing with controlled descents began to gain popularity.

The new developments also prompted interest in New Zealand, Alaska, and California. In the California gold fields in the middle of the last century skiing was encouraged by a remarkable man. In his native Norway, his name had been John Torteinson, but when he came to America to dig for his fortune, he changed it to John Thompson.

He soon became known as "Snowshoe Thompson." Actually, it was skis, not snowshoes that earned his fame, but most of the miners had never seen skis before, and when Thompson slid into their camps they called the things snowshoes.

When snowfall closed down the mines, Thompson taught his friends how to make and use skis. Downhill racing soon became immensely popular. Challenges between rival camps with large wagers sparked the interest.

The races did not call for fancy turns. The courses ran straight down steep slopes. Speeds were incredible. In Plumas County, one miner set a record of eighty-seven miles an hour on a 1,804-foot drop and survived to brag about it. He may have exaggerated a bit as well, because such speed is unheard of in modern Alpine racing.

Thompson himself won many races, but he earned his fame and the affection of fellow miners as a skiing postman. Through the long winter months, Thompson often provided the only contact with the outside world. Usually he carried medicine and other vital supplies as well as the mail.

His route led ninety miles over the Sierra. He could cover the distance in five days, but often he was delayed breaking trail to some isolated camp or helping rescue teams search for lost men.

His confidence, skill, independence, and daring set a standard in the Old West that is still recalled with pride. Ironically, Thompson went to his grave without ever collecting the full pay due on his government mail contract. And his pioneer work as an ambassador of skiing did not produce lasting results. When the gold gave out and the miners left the hills, skiing in America was all but forgotten.

In the European Alps, however, the sport gained ground steadily. Ski instruction became a respected occupation. Soldiers were trained to ski. The downhill slalom was devised to raise competition to a high level.

Alpine resorts for vacationing skiers, particularly English skiers, met with success. Thus by the beginning of this century, skiing was a major sport in Europe. Scandinavians specialized in cross-country racing and jumping, both of which became known as Nordic skiing, while those in Alpine countries specialized in downhill and slalom racing, known simply as Alpine skiing.

In America, with a few skiing clubs and some rustic ski camps, the sport received little public attention. But then came the 1932 Winter Olympics at New York's Lake Placid.

European skiers put on a dazzling show that was de-

scribed in the newspapers and over national radio net-
works. Interest boomed. Resorts were soon being built in
mountain regions all across the continent, and resort owners imported some of the best European skiers as instruc-
tors.

The sport has continued to grow steadily until today's
Americans are often a match for the best Europeans in
both Nordic and Alpine skiing.

While resorts offer competition at many levels, most
weekend skiers find plenty of satisfaction without it. Prac-
ticing skills on the slopes or traveling cross-country through
the mountains is exciting enough. This explains in great
part the attraction of the sport. Anyone with legs and a fair
sense of balance can participate and have fun.

Skates may have been invented before skis, but no ancient
samples of skates have been unearthed to give any firm evidence of age. Written mention of skating first appears in
two thousand-year-old Norse records which describe bone
runners tied to the feet with thongs.

These skates were probably fashioned from rib bones
of reindeer. Although trimmed and polished, they could
hardly have been given the edge necessary for precise turns.

Like skis, skates at first were simply practical implements of travel. As such, they had greatest use in areas
where there was either a man-made or natural system of
waterways. Holland with its many canals was ideal. The
Dutch, in fact, claim credit for the invention of skating,
and the claim may have merit, but it is quite likely that
skating was independently discovered in different regions.

Siberian natives probably were using walrus tusk
skates and the Chinese were gliding across the ice on skates
of tightly bound cornstalks at about the same time that the
Dutch were tying bone runners on their shoes.

Although they were mainly practical implements, skates soon became tools of pleasure to some. We have this description from a twelfth century English writer:

"When the great fenne or moore is frozen, many young men play on the yce. . . . Some tye bones on their feet and under their helles, and shoving themselves by a little picked staffe, so slide swiftly as a bird flyeth in the aire, or an arrow out of a crossbow."

A favorite scene for Dutch painters of the fourteenth century was the frozen canal covered with skaters. While many of the skaters seem to be shopping, running errands, or speeding on their way to work, some obviously are simply out to have a good time.

The skates shown in these paintings are carved from wood. Wooden skates, which can be given a sharper edge than bone, showed a significant improvement. Undoubtedly young Siedwi was wearing wooden skates when she suffered a bad fall on the ice in 1396. Her injuries left her crippled for life, but the plucky Dutch lass never complained. In fact, she bore her troubles with so much fortitude and good spirit that she was made a saint soon after her death.

Wooden skates were clumsy looking, but they were still a great improvement over the bone runners worn by the first skaters.

Siedwi, the patron saint of skating, was injured in a fall, in 1396, but she never complained. Instead, she devoted her life to helping others.

So skating is one of the few sports to have a patron saint, and it is fitting that she was a Dutch girl.

Skating for pleasure increased greatly when iron skates were introduced late in the eighteenth century. Then clamps replaced bindings. A skate that could be given a knife edge and held firmly on the foot advanced skating to an art.

Racing was the first ice competition, but it was soon followed by the invention of a team sport. Ice hockey was introduced by a group of British soldiers who were stationed in Canada in the 1860s. The soldiers simply transferred the rules and strategy of field hockey to the ice. The game was adopted by Canadians with zeal and became their national game. Now an Olympic event, ice hockey, the world's fastest team sport, is played by many nations on both amateur and professional levels.

About the time ice hockey was invented, skaters of more artistic taste and temperament began experimenting with figure skating. The metal, clamp-on skates made precision moves possible, moves that had all the grace of ballet.

Jackson Haines, an American dancing teacher, recognized the similarities between figure skating and ballet, and during a visit to Europe, began teaching dancing moves to young skaters. The Haines technique and style spread through Europe and then to America as competitive figure skating gained popularity.

Steel skates that screw to the soles of special boots have replaced the old clamp-ons, but the Haines teaching methods still influence instruction for today's young figure skaters.

While figure skating and hockey are the most popular of ice sports, there are other games that enjoy regional support. Not the least of these is curling, a sport closely allied with bowling, the subject of the next chapter.

Chapter Ten

Variations on a Theme

Bowling, if not one of the oldest games, has certainly appeared through the years with the most variations. While today's tenpins, lawn bowling, and curling on the ice are all based on the same principle, they are distinctly different games.

And it seems that bowling was independently invented in different lands and different eras.

Polynesians who lived in Pacific isolation for centuries played *Ula Maika* by rolling elliptical stones at target sticks. By strange coincidence, the sticks were placed sixty feet away from the bowler. The modern bowling alley is sixty feet long.

Native Americans in the snowy regions of North America had a game called snow snake. The object was to see how far a stone, spear, or dart could be scooted along a prepared track in the snow. Although this was not a target

Though not a target game, snow snake, common among Indians of North America, called for a prepared track or lane in the snow and a strong underhand throw.

game like most other forms of bowling, it has to be included as a variation on the theme.

And there were a host of native American games that did test the aim. These ranged from the simple children's pastime of throwing stones at a disc hung in a tree to the dart and hoop game, which was both difficult to play and complex in religious overtones.

The goal was to hit a rolling hoop or disk with an arrow, spear, or dart. Among most tribes, the hoop was loosely woven with a pattern of intersecting strands that marked special scoring spots. If a dart struck a small circle or square woven in the pattern, for instance, it counted more than one that struck outside this mark.

For some groups, the hoop represented a magic shield and the game was played as a sham war. For others, the hoop represented the sun and the missiles thrown at it represented watersnakes, symbolic of the source of life. For at least one tribe, the disk stood for the web of the spider woman, mother of the twin gods of war, and the darts were the gods themselves.

The game was often part of the ritual marking the opening of the harvest or the start of the salmon run. Hitting the hoop meant a successful harvest or good fishing.

The Micmacs of Nova Scotia and the Zuni and the Navajo of the Southwest threw hoops at stakes set as far apart as accurate throws were possible. Like modern quoits and horseshoes, the object was to score ringers or at least place the hoops closer than the opponent's.

Eskimos pitched disks at hides placed about ten feet apart. Each player, throwing from one hide to the other, had five bone disks, and the object was to place them on or as close as possible to marker disks placed in the center of each hide. This was a gambling game, and it was not unusual for a man to bet all he owned on one turn with the tossing disks.

The Haidas of Alaska's Prince of Wales Island played a stone toss game with a stone pin as a target. The first player to knock the pin down ten times was the winner. The first American bowling game? You might call it that.

The oldest bowling equipment yet known was found in the tomb of an Egyptian boy who died in about 5200 B.C. Among the funeral objects were a collection of stones, some round and others pointed with flat bases. The round stones, archeologists believe, were meant to be rolled at the pointed ones that may have been set up much like pins in a modern bowling alley.

The Egyptian find, however, is an isolated one. Nothing has since been discovered to suggest that the game was common in Egypt or that it influenced development of bowling or bowling-related games among neighboring people.

Today's game of tenpins has German roots that have been traced back to about 300 A.D., long after the boy bowler of Egypt died.

It was the custom for all males of Germanic tribes to carry clubs or *kegels* to settle any arguments that might come up with man or beast. A club in the hands of a hot-head was a serious threat for the priests and missionaries who struggled to Christianize Germany.

The priests ordered that all clubs be stacked at the door whenever the men entered a place of worship. The club, the priests said, was evil, and leaving it at the door was an act of faith and peace.

To carry this symbolism a step further, the priests invented a game. When a man came to church, he was given a round stone to roll at his club. If the man could knock down the "evil" club, the priest praised him for his virtue.

A stone ball and "pins" found in the 5200 B.C. tomb of an Egyptian boy are the oldest known bowling relics.

If the man failed to knock the club over, he was warned to correct his sinful ways.

The game at first was undoubtedly taken quite seriously, but eventually kegling, as bowling is still sometimes called today, was pursued for fun, with the religious overtones forgotten.

Bowling became a regular part of festivals and celebrations in every German community. Even the smallest villages had a place for bowling. It was a poor tavern that did not offer bowling to its patrons. And every rich man's estate of consequence had a place to bowl.

Over the centuries, the game spread to the Netherlands and France, then to the Scandinavian countries, England, and Scotland. Rules and equipment varied. In some regions the target pins were sharp sticks stuck in the ground. In other regions, the target was a smaller ball, and the object was to bowl as close as possible to the small ball without hitting it.

The variations led to other distinct games that gave origin to the modern sports such as shuffleboard, the Italian bocci, lawn bowling which became so popular in Great Britain and its colonies, and curling on the ice now played with enthusiasm in Scotland and Scandinavia.

The most popular form of the game, however, remained bowling on a lane of grass or packed ground at a group of kegels. At first the kegels were arranged in a diamond pattern, and the goal was to knock down all but the center kegel.

For a long time, there was no agreement on the number of kegels that could be used. In some games, as many as fifteen were set up at the end of the alley.

It was Martin Luther, the religious reformer and bowling enthusiast, who is credited with standardizing the rules. He said that nine pins, no more and no less, should be used in the target pattern. Ninepins, as it became known, was soon being played throughout Europe on an alley sixty feet in length. And it was the game of ninepins that Dutch settlers brought with them to the New World.

New York City's Bowling Green was set aside by the Dutch for their popular game, but this was not the only place to bowl in the colonies. The game spread to many regions, becoming almost as popular as it was in Europe.

For the puritan churchman of the day, the game was too popular. Considering the religious origins of bowling, this was an ironic twist, but the churchmen had a point. American sportsmen bet heavily on ninepins, and tempting wagers led to cheating. The game soon attracted the lowest elements of society.

The result was that many communities outlawed the game. Both New York and Connecticut adopted laws banning ninepins with stiff penalties for anyone caught playing the game.

Owners of lanes quickly found a loophole. They changed the game by adding another pin. There were no laws banning tenpins. So bowling and the heavy betting that went with it continued. The pattern of pins was changed from a diamond to a triangle, and indoor lanes allowed bowling to gain status as a year-round sport.

But the taint on bowling remained. The bowling alley was often a haven for the riffraff of the community. It was not until 1895, when the American Bowling Congress was formed that conditions began to change. With the support of alley owners, the bad name that the game had acquired was eventually erased. Today, bowling is a favorite family sport.

In America alone, it is estimated that some forty million people go bowling each year. The sport is alive and well. Its future is bright.

PART II

Team
Games

Chapter Eleven

Play Ball

Scholars tell us that the first ball may have been a human head kicked about by warriors celebrating victory over a hapless and headless foe.

Perhaps there is symbolic satisfaction to be gained by kicking the head of an enemy, but there were undoubtedly other, less grisly, balls for the ancients to play with. What these balls were made of determined the nature of play.

A ball of stone or wood, for instance, would be too hard and heavy to kick. It would have to be carried, thrown, or rolled. On the other hand, a ball made of an inflated animal bladder would be ideal for a kicking game.

Although our modern games of basketball, rugby, football, baseball, and soccer have complex strategy and rules, it would be a mistake to regard them as entirely new games.

In China, during the Han Dynasty which lasted from 207 B.C. to 220 A.D., there were two kinds of ball-kicking games. In one, players took turns kicking a ball at a target. In the other, players took turns showing off their skill in juggling, dribbling, and passing the ball without touching it with their hands, similar to today's practice drill for soccer.

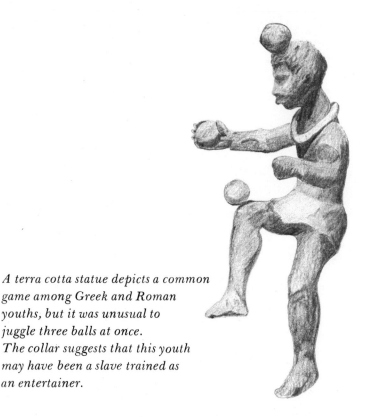

A terra cotta statue depicts a common game among Greek and Roman youths, but it was unusual to juggle three balls at once. The collar suggests that this youth may have been a slave trained as an entertainer.

Japan's *kemari* is at least fourteen hundred years old. A ceremonial game, it is played by eight men who stand in a fourteen-meter square. A tree marks each corner of the square. The players pass the ball with their feet, taking care to keep it always within the boundaries of the square.

With a ball and stick, Egyptians held batting contests as early as 5000 B.C. And although we cannot be sure how complex these contests became, the Egyptians were inventive people. There may well have been fielders who tried to catch the batted ball on the fly.

The Greeks, we know, were not inclined to play team games, but a ball promotes teamwork. In the *Odyssey*, Homer described the mythical islands of Phaiacia where maidens danced with a purple ball, tossing it to and fro with graceful coordination and in time with their song.

Greeks used balls in their gymnasiums to improve balance and agility. Lifting a ball on the foot, and then from the knee to the head was apparently a standard part of individual exercise with a ball.

A fourth century B.C. bas-relief found in Athens shows a youth either balancing or lofting a ball off his thigh while holding both hands behind him. A younger boy nearby watches the performance with obvious admiration. It was also a challenge to bounce a ball off a wall, keeping it aloft with head, shoulders, or knees, but without the use of hands.

Sophocles and Alexander the Great were reportedly experts at this form of ball play.

Catch with two or more players had many variations. Egyptian wall paintings show girl acrobats catching a ball as they ride piggyback. A similar scene with male athletes is depicted on a Greek vase dating back to the sixth century B.C. And a wall painting in Pompeii shows cupids playing the piggyback game.

The Greeks called this popular sport *ephedrismos*. It may have been a form of keep-away because the three or

The game of ephedrismos *appears to have been piggyback keep-away. When a player dropped a throw or made a bad one, he had to change places with his "horse."*

more pairs of players are always shown. Under the rules, when a rider dropped the ball, he or she changed places with the partner to become the horse.

Players in simple games of catch, popular with the Greeks and Romans, were eliminated after they had dropped or mishandled the ball a specified number of times. An individual could play this game alone by bouncing the ball off the wall as long as possible without a miscue.

Although Romans as a rule would rather watch than participate in sports, they made an exception for ball games. Nearly every villa had a ball room or court where the wealthy Roman and his guests could work up a sweat or an appetite juggling and bouncing balls.

The Romans also had a three-man game called Trigon. The players, standing on points of a triangle, tried to pass or punch the ball from one man to the next without letting it fall to the ground.

Despite the Greek resistance to team sports, the young men of Sparta played a team ball game with enthusiasm. Spartan inscriptions record the victories of the teams at regular meets, and Spartan boys in their first year of manhood were referred to as ballplayers. Participation in the game was apparently a mandatory part of Spartan military training.

The prize for the winning team was a sickle, and the winners were apparently determined on a tournament system because the inscriptions speak of some teams drawing a bye. There were at least fifteen players on a side, and the game was played on a field marked with boundaries. But no further details of the game have survived.

Some scholars have contended that it was the game of *platanistas*. This we know was played on a field bounded by water-filled ditches. The object was to trip, push, kick, or wrestle the opponents off the field into the water. Play may have looked at times like a modern football or rugby contest, but there is no mention of a ball being used in *platanistas*.

Scholars of rugby sometimes claim the ancient game of *harpastum* for the original of their sport. But from what little we know about it, *harpastum* seems to have been a refinement of the game of keep-away.

Apollinaris Sidonius, a fifth century A.D. Latin writer who became a Christian saint, said that the game had a midrunner which suggests keep-away. Sidonius described dice playing and *harpastum* as the two most popular pastimes of his day and said that wealthy landowners of Gaul had courts where the game was played. According to Sidonius, guests would line up waiting their turns at the game. This does not suggest a team sport.

A much earlier mention of *harpastum* comes from a fragment attributed to the fourth century B.C. Greek poet, Antiphanes, who described the actions of an expert.

"When he got the ball he delighted to give it to one player while dodging the other; he knocked it away from one and urged on another with noisy cries . . . 'outside, a long pass, beyond him, over his head, a short pass . . .' "

The origins of rugby seem closer to two other Greek games. One was called *episkyros* or *epikoinos* and was described by the second century A.D. grammarian Julius Pollux. The other was an unnamed game mentioned by the Greek physician Galen in the same century.

Galen, in listing healthy exercises, said that several players can take part in a sport with a small ball. Players surround the ball, and each tries to keep the others from taking possession of it. This suggests the scrimmage of modern day rugby.

Pollux tells us that *episkyros* was a team game played on a field marked with a center line and two end lines. The

The bas-relief showing what may be the game of episkyros *is the only illustration that has survived of a Greek team sport. It looks as if the players could not start running until the ball was in the air.*

team that possessed the ball tried to throw it beyond their opponents. Those on the other team tried to catch the ball and throw it back. The object was to outthrow the other team so that one would eventually be forced back over its own end line.

The game, according to Pollux, was popular with teenage boys, and this suggests that *episkyros* may have been the game that was played by Spartan youth at an earlier time.

Episkyros or a game very much like it was still being played in 600 A.D., the date of a bas-relief unearthed in Athens in 1920. The stone carving depicts six athletes, three on a side, with one of them preparing to throw a ball. Those on the side opposing him appear ready to make a catch while other members of the thrower's team seem ready to run.

The carving, incidentally, is the only illustration found so far of a Greek team sport.

Greeks and Romans made balls by stitching together strips of leather cut to form a sphere. The Romans played with three different types. The smallest was stuffed with hair and like the game of keep-away was called *harpastum*. A larger ball, stuffed with feathers, was called a *pila,* and the largest ball of all, a *follis,* may have enclosed an inflated air bladder.

If the *follis* was a light, air-inflated ball, it would have been ideal for kicking, but there is no record of a Roman kicking game. Some scholars have suggested, just the same, that Roman soldiers who invaded the British Isles introduced the forerunner of both soccer and rugby.

It seems more likely, however, that the kicking game that became so popular in England was a home-grown product. Indeed, there may be some truth to the claim that a crude form of rugby was being played there as far back as the Bronze Age.

Early historic accounts mention a game particularly popular in Cornwall where a ball was thrown, kicked, or carried between goals that were sometimes four miles apart.

Players could trip, shove, hit, wrestle, or use any other means to gain control of the ball. Use of weapons, however, was apparently discouraged. Contests sometimes lasted a full day. A similar game, called *La Soule,* was popular across the English Channel in Normandy.

From time to time, through the centuries, efforts were made to ban the game. The players not only injured each other but they also trampled crops, frightened livestock, and broke down gates and fences. Innocent bystanders were often drawn into the game over their protests. But the prohibitions did not have much effect, at least not in England. The game thrived.

Even monarchs, including Edward II and III, Richard II, Henry VIII, and Elizabeth I, tried to ban the game because it was causing neglect of archery. But the ball game went on.

Sir Thomas Elyot said in 1531 that the game was "nothing but beastly fury and extreme violence." Elyot recommended that the game be "put in perpetual silence." But hotter heads prevailed.

Whole parishes played against each other, and the biggest contests were held on Shrove Tuesday, the last day before Lent. An account of the game in 1602 said that the players "take their way over hills, dales, hedges, ditches, yea and throw bushes, briars, mires, plashes, and rivers whatsoever, so you shall sometimes see twenty or thirty lie tugging together in the water, scrambling and scratching for the ball."

Unable to prevent the game, responsible citizens apparently took the next best step and tried to control it with rules intended to reduce injury and encourage fair play.

Controls clearly did not take effect overnight, but the game eventually gained enough respectability to enter the schoolyard. By the early 1800s, English schoolboys were playing a primitive form of rugby. The field had fixed boundaries, but it would sometimes be crowded with as many as 300 players.

The ball could be kicked only. A player could not pick it up and run with it. Even holding it called for restart of play.

Rugby enthusiasts point to one William Webb Ellis as the hero of their game. He, according to legend, was the first to run with the ball in a match played at Rugby Public School. Although Ellis cannot be found on the student rolls, it is certain that the school gave the modern game of rugby its name. And in 1846, the school published the first rules of the new game.

The rules, making it legal to run with the ball, did not sit well with advocates of the kicking game. Thus a division arose. The division was formalized by the creation in 1863 of the Football Association.

From that point on, sportsmen either played rugby or association football. The word "association" was eventually shortened and changed to "soccer."

In America, schoolboys played a game modeled after association football until a historic game in 1874 between Harvard and McGill universities when rugby rules were followed. American football is said to have originated with this game, but actually games played with modified rugby rules soon after gave the American sport its true beginnings.

One of the most significant modifications came in 1880, when the rugby scrum was replaced with the scrimmage line as a starting point for each play. A team was given three downs to make five yards, but this, as we know was soon changed as were many other rules until we now have the unique game of American football.

Chapter Twelve

Lacrosse

In Athens, not far from the sixth century bas-relief carving depicting six ball players, another wall carving came to light. It showed a different game.

In this carving two young men holding curved sticks face each other over a ball. The scene suggests the face-off in a modern game of field hockey, and field hockey or something much like it certainly belongs in the ranks of ancient sports.

Although the Greeks played a ball and stick game and probably passed it on to the Romans, it was most likely invented by the Persians and Indians to the East. Roman soldiers may have introduced the game to the British Islands, but some scholars say that the Irish were playing a ball and stick game called hurley more than a thousand years before the Roman invasion.

Hurley actually may have been the crude rugby-like game described in the last chapter. When a ball of soft material or an air bladder was used, the ball could be kicked. But if nothing softer than a wooden ball was available, then the players carried sticks.

Certainly a ball and stick is a natural combination for play. It was such a popular combination in North America that it would have been fair at one time to have called it a "national sport."

Native Americans from coast to coast had refined the ball and stick game to a high level long before the first European explorers arrived.

With further refinements, European settlers would eventually convert the native game into what we know today as lacrosse. The modern game, however, is quite different from the native sport.

For one thing, the native game seemed to be remarkably free of rules. Although seventy players on a side was the average number, there were times when teams of two thousand or more took the field. The field itself might be a mile or more long, and dimensions might change during a game.

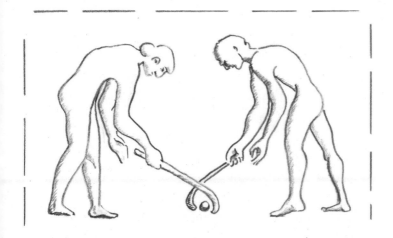

A 600 A.D. bas-relief from Greece shows a face-off with ball and sticks that is not unlike modern field hockey. Although several players apparently took turns vying for the ball, this probably was not a team game.

For some tribes, the medicine men served as "goal posts." If they wandered about during the course of the afternoon as they often did then the battle wandered with them.

Another thing that makes the native game difficult to compare with its modern form is that each tribe had its own variation of play. In some areas, a player carried two webbed sticks and used them like tongs to handle the ball. In other areas, a single stick was used.

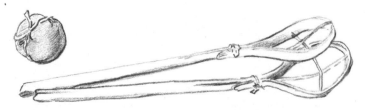

Sticks used by the Seminole Indians of Florida were thirteen inches long. The ball was two-and-a-quarter inches in diameter.

Among some tribes, throwing the ball with the hands was permitted provided that the ball had first been caught or picked up with the webbing. Among other tribes the rules banned ball handling in any form. If a player should put his hands on the ball, the game was stopped and re-started from the center of the field.

In all areas, betting on the outcome of the game was heavy. Highly valued possessions, including bowls, baskets, blankets, and even horses were wagered. And though again varying from tribe to tribe, the ritual that accompanied the game was observed with unswerving faith everywhere.

The game was part of a religious rite. James Mooney who lived with the Cherokee in the late 1880s saw the ball and stick game was an essential part of their life.

The Cherokee believed that the first game was played between the birds and the ground animals of the forest. Long before man came to the forest, according to Cherokee myth, the animals challenged the birds to a ball game. The birds accepted the challenge and prepared for the match. At the agreed spot for the game, the animals gathered on the ground while the birds perched in the trees.

While waiting for the game to start, two small creatures climbed in the trees and pleaded for a chance to play. The animals, thinking them too small to be of use, had already turned them down. The birds also thought the creatures too small, and besides they had four legs and should be on the animal team.

Just the same the birds felt sorry for the creatures. So for one of them they took the skin from a drum and fashioned two wings for the little thing to hold in its front paws. The wings worked wonderfully, and the little creature was soon swooping and darting about with amazing speed. Thus the bat was created.

There was no drum skin left to make wings for the other creature so the birds tugged at its body with their beaks, stretching the skin along each side between its legs. And this was how the flying squirrel came to be.

When the game began, the squirrel sailed down from a limb, picked up the ball, and carried it into the trees for the birds. They kept it in the air for some time, but then the ball dropped.

Just before it fell into the paws of the animals, however, the bat swooped down and recovered it. He dodged so well and flew so swiftly that none of the animals could reach the ball. The bat flew to the goal and won the game for the birds.

Because of the help from the bat and squirrel, the Cherokee ball player always invoked their aid before every game. And it was a common practice for a player to tie a small piece of bat wing to his stick as a luck charm.

Mooney reported that during the ball playing season from midsummer to late fall, Cherokee men trained constantly. Practice usually continued each day until dark.

Matches were arranged between neighboring tribes after one had challenged the other. At least two weeks prior to a match, the players were placed under strict tabu. They could not eat rabbit because it was a timid animal. They could not eat frog meat because a frog's bones were brittle. The young of any bird and certain fish and herbs were also banned.

A player was not allowed to touch a woman before and for several days after a game. And if a woman should ever touch a player's stick, it was believed that every member of the team would lose his skill and be defeated. This tabu against women was common wherever the game was played.

The head medicine man of the tribe prepared the players for the game with a variety of special rites. Chief among these was the water rite. For this the player waded into a lake or stream and stood facing away from shore while the medicine man, standing behind him, performed a symbolic ritual with pebbles.

As game day approached, the medicine man became the busiest member of the tribe. He performed the water rite not just once but several times for each member of the team. In the minds of the players, the contest would be a struggle between rival medicine men. The one with the most powerful magic would be able to make his team win.

Every bit of magic was used during the tribal rally the night before the game.

The players, who had been fasting all day, gathered at the rally place at sundown. The place had to be close to water and was usually on the route to the playing field.

After several bonfires were lit, the players began dancing in the purifying smoke of the largest fire.

Meanwhile the medicine man sprinkled trails leading to the dancing ground with rabbit stew. This prevented the magic of the rival tribe from reaching the dancers.

All the tribe took part in the ritual, and soon after dawn they began the march to the playing ground. Many stops were made along the way to repeat the water rite. The medicine man also delivered a pep talk, telling the players how great their wealth will be when they collect the winnings after their victory.

On arriving at the playing field, the medicine man used a stick to sketch a small plan of the field on the ground. Then he marked the position of each player with a small stake.

Next, the players were scratched with a special comb with seven, needle-sharp points made of split turkey bones. The comb was passed four times down the length of each arm and then four times in a crossing pattern on the player's back and chest. No player showed any sign of pain during this ordeal, but the scratches were deep enough to draw blood.

The Cherokee playing outfit was simple, just a breechcloth tied with a thin thong that would break should an opponent try to hold it. The headdress was more complex. It usually combined eagle feathers for keen eyesight, a deer's tail for swiftness, and a snake rattle to terrify the enemy.

Finally, after decorating their scratched bodies with paint and charcoal from the previous night's fire the men were ready to play. But before either team took the field, all men went to the shore for one last water rite.

It was early afternoon by the time all preparations had been finished and the medicine man from each team led his players in single file onto the field. Both sides of the field were lined with spectators. The goals at either end consisted of two upright poles.

The ball, furnished by the challengers, was about the size of a tennis ball, made of deer hide stuffed with deer hair. It was tossed in the air in the center of the field, and the game finally began. The players crushed together, each one trying to catch the ball in his stick. There was so much pushing, however, that the ball most often fell to the ground.

As soon as a player picked it up, he began running toward the opponent's goal. The defenders, racing to keep up with the ball carrier, hit him with their sticks or tried to trip him. "Almost everything short of murder is allowable in the game, and both parties sometimes go into the contest with the deliberate purpose of crippling or otherwise disabling the best players on the opposing side."

The better players were able to keep the ball in the air, passing it to a teammate just before being intercepted by a defender, always working the ball toward the goal.

The medicine men did not watch the action. They hid near the shore, using all the magic they knew to influence the outcome of play.

Whenever one side managed to hurl the ball between the poles to score a goal, the game was restarted with a toss-up at the center of the field. For the Cherokee, the first team to score twelve goals won the game. Other tribes had different rules. For some, play continued until sundown, and the team having the most goals at that time won.

At the end of the game, the winners went at once to the water where the medicine man performed more magic to prevent any harm from revengeful spirits of the losers. Next came a feast provided by the squaws. During the feast, wagers were settled with the winners collecting their stakes:

the losers usually challenged the winners to another match. When the time and place was agreed upon, all returned to their villages to prepare for the return engagement.

In Canada, where the ball and stick game was known as baggataway, the native Americans used it to trick the English garrison at Fort Mackinaw in 1763. Allies of the recently defeated French, the natives were still not trusted by the English soldiers, but on June 4, the soldiers relaxed their guard.

It was King George's birthday, and the native Americans themselves suggested a ball game to celebrate the occasion. Play began in a field before the gates of the fort. Most of the soldiers came out to watch. Some began betting. They forgot that they were seriously outnumbered by the hundreds of Indians who had turned out for the game.

On a signal, one player sent the ball bounding toward the fort gates. All the players rushed after it. In the confusion, the squaws joined the melee. They passed weapons hidden beneath their blankets to the braves.

As soon as the natives were armed, the killing began. The soldiers had no time to organize a defense. The fort was overrun. Only a few settlers escaped to tell the story of the game that turned into a massacre.

A century later, the game played a part in a minor campaign of the Civil War. A confederate detachment, made up of Cherokees, was assigned the job of guarding a bridge across the Holston River in Tennessee. Bored by the job, the men soon began cutting willow sticks for a game of ball.

The game was in full rush when Union troops arrived, burned the bridge, and sent the Cherokees running. Reports suggest that some of the natives were true sportsmen, more upset by the inability to finish the game than by the loss of the bridge.

It was the game of baggataway that was adopted by French settlers. Because the sticks looked to the French like bishops' croziers, the settlers called the game lacrosse. In 1876, Canadian teams introduced the sport in England with demonstration matches.

With some modifications, the game was taken up with enthusiasm by English women who eventually promoted it in the United States. The Woman's Lacrosse Association was formed here in 1931.

For men, lacrosse clubs became active in most of New England. The cities of New York and Baltimore became centers for competition. Colleges began playing the game late in the last century. Princeton, Harvard, and Yale were among the first schools to field teams. The Intercollegiate Lacrosse Association, however, was not formed until 1926.

Although interest still centers in eastern states, the National Collegiate Athletic Association now sponsors an annual tournament open to the eight best teams in the nation. With this support, interest in lacrosse is sure to grow. The game may soon again be played from coast to coast.

Chapter Thirteen

The Court Game

When the world began, according to Maya legend, the only light came from Arara, the god with the face of fire.

There was no sun, moon, or stars. Plants and animals thrived, but people did not inhabit the earth until the twins, Hun and Vucub, came down from heaven.

They played a game with a rubber ball. Because the noise of the constantly bouncing ball bothered the gods of the underworld, they plotted against the playful twins. Thus the struggle between the forces of light and darkness began.

The gods of the underworld sent four owls to the twins, challenging them to a ball game in the underworld. Hun and Vucub accepted the challenge, but they did not trust the gods fully. So they left the rubber ball behind, hidden in their heavenly home.

Of course, it was a trick. There was no ball game. Instead the gods put the twins on trial and executed them by cutting out their hearts, chopping off their heads, and throwing their bodies on a rubbish heap.

Hun's head was spiked on a barren tree by the road-

side where all the underworld could see it and rejoice in
the power of darkness. But the forces of light began fighting back.

The barren tree bloomed and bore fruit. This frightened the gods of the underworld. No one, they said, shall
ever come near the tree. But a young girl, the daughter of
a prince, was curious. Like Eve, she was tempted by the
fruit.

When she approached the tree, foam from the mouth
of Hun's head fell on her hand. The girl conceived. When
word of this miracle reached the gods of darkness, they
banished the girl.

Driven from the underworld, she went to the heavenly
home of the twins' mother who welcomed her. Soon the
girl gave birth to twin boys, Hunahpu and Xbalanque.
While growing up the boys discovered the hidden ball and
began to play the game.

Again the gods of the underworld sent a challenge,
but this time Hunahpu and Xbalanque outwitted them.
They killed the gods and took over the underworld and the
earth. They recovered the bodies of Hun and Vucub and
placed them in the sky as the sun and the moon.

The Maya believed that as long as the ball game was
played night would follow day and day follow night. The
sun and the moon would continue in their courses, rising
and setting just as the heavenly twins ordained.

And this was why man played a game with a rubber
ball.

For years, archeologists have been searching for the
less fanciful origins of the ancient ball game. They have
not had much luck. In fact, archeologists are still uncer-
tain how the game was played.

The Maya called it pok-to-pok because of the sound
the rubber ball made when it bounced off the walls of the

A Maya carving shows a ball player wearing protective belt and helmet, necessary when playing with a solid rubber ball that weighed up to five pounds.

court. Hitting the opponent's wall may have been an important part of the game. It is fairly certain that possession of the ball could be retained only as long as one team was able to keep it in the air. This alone was difficult because the players were not allowed to use their hands.

With the teams facing each other, each with a long wall of the court behind it, it is easy to imagine those players with the ball as the offensive team and the others as defenders of their wall.

But there is no evidence supporting this vision of how pok-to-pok was played. There is, however, evidence on many other aspects of the game.

Perhaps the most startling thing about the court game was its wide popularity. It was played from the Amazon Valley of South America, where some believe it may have begun, all the way to the deserts of Arizona. It was played in the highlands of Mexico, the mountains of Guatemala, the plains of the Yucatan Peninsula, and the islands of the Caribbean.

Natives with different languages and different cultures often held nothing in common but the ball game. Among sophisticated cultures such as the Mayan, Aztec, Toltec, and Hohokam the game was played in a walled court.

In less developed areas, it was apparently played in the village plazas or any other open area that was convenient. For the Maya, it seems clear, the game began as a religious ritual, as important as prayer and sacrifice. And it was played for high stakes.

Winners had the right to go among the crowd collecting robes and jewelry from the spectators. Losers sometimes lost their heads in a ceremony of sacrifice following the game.

Reports by Spanish conquistadors suggest that sacrifice was common following the Aztec ball game. Cortez's men say a rack beside the ball court of Tenochitlan (site of today's Mexico City) displayed the bloody heads of one hundred and thirty-six thousand sacrificial victims. The figure is hard to believe. The Toltecs, whose civilization flowered before the Aztecs, reportedly beheaded the captain of the losing team.

The Maya, whose civilization began well before both the Toltecs and the Aztecs, were generally not as blood-thirsty, but the ball game was certainly of high importance. In the territory of the Maya, embracing Guatemala, Yucatan, and Chiapas, archeologists have found and identified forty-five ball courts.

Chichén Itzá, one of the largest of Mayan ceremonial cities, had seven courts including a huge one that embraced a field 120 feet wide and 480 feet long. The more common size was about thirty by fifty feet.

The walls bordering the courts were about eight-and-a-half feet high. Sometimes they enclosed the court completely, but usually the ends of the playing field were left open.

Early Spanish observers reported that the oldest court

In the Mexican highlands at Mount Alban, near the modern city of Oaxaca, the largest court was open at one end and closed at the other.

found at that time is in western Honduras at the Mayan city of Copán. The rectangular field is bordered by sloping walls of cut stone that lead up to stone verticals. Large parrot heads carved in stone mark the junction of the sloped with the vertical walls. There are six heads in all, three on each wall.

The ends of this stone-paved court are open, but the paving extends several feet beyond the walls. The north-south orientation of the court is typical of other courts found in the region.

Archeologists say the court was built about 600 A.D.

The same type of court continued to be built until about 1000 A.D. in the lowlands of Maya territory. To the south in the highlands of Guatemala, the Maya built a different type. Oriented in an east-west direction, these courts were walled in at the ends, making a complete enclosure.

Sometime after 1000 A.D. these early models gave way to two other types. One type, found both in southern Mexico and the Guatemala highlands, was made by excavation. Although the court floor was below ground level, in most other respects it resembled earlier models. But it did not have carvings along the walls. The second new type, found in southern Mexico and the flatlands of Yucatan, was built with vertical rather than sloping walls. It is in these courts that a stone ring set vertically in each wall first appeared.

The openings in these rings was not much larger than the circumference of the ball, but it seems that extra points could be won by sending the ball through the ring. This must certainly have been a rare feat. Not only were the players prevented from handling the ball, but they also were weighed down with padding worn on hips and knees. The padding was necessary to soften the impact of the ball, which was made of solid rubber and weighed about five pounds.

Archeologists still cannot agree on the origin of the stone ring. Some think it developed in the Yucatan region of the Maya and spread into southern Mexico, while others suggest that the ring was a Toltec idea that was brought to the Yucatan when the Toltec invaded Maya territory.

More puzzling has been the discovery of ball courts in the Arizona desert, the only courts found north of present-day Mexico City. At first these sunken courts of Arizona were thought to have had something to do with sun worship, but they have since been identified as ball courts with sloping walls and midcourt markers similar to the courts of Yucatan and Mexico.

Almost sixty Arizona courts have been found. Some are large depressions closed at the ends and oriented in an east-west direction. The best example of this type is at the ruins of Snaketown. The second type, called a Casa Grande court, is smaller, oriented north-south with an opening in each end.

The larger courts were probably built between 800 and 900 A.D. The smaller courts were built later, between 900 and 1150 A.D.

All were built by the Hohokam, a people who were linked by trade with the well-developed civilizations of Mexico, Yucatan, and Guatemala.

The trade route was a long one. The discovery in 1924 of a rubber ball at Arizona's Casa Grande shows that the route led at least to the tropical jungles of Central America, the closest source of rubber.

In active use from about 700 to 900 A.D., perhaps much longer, the route apparently followed the Pacific Coast. This seems the best explanation for the lack of discovery in central Mexico between Arizona and Mexico City. No trace of a ball court has yet been found in this vast region.

Investigation of early Hohokam and Mayan ruins suggests that extensive religious ritual accompanied the game. The oldest courts have been found only among the ruins of large settlements where a full staff of priests was available for ritual.

Later, toward the decline of the Maya and the Hohokam, the situation changed. Courts were built in small towns. Archeologists believe this shows a decline in the religious importance of the game. But there were many other reasons to play.

The Aztecs played the game to settle political disputes, give an excuse for betting, and provide exciting competition between villages.

On the Caribbean islands, a court game played between teams of ten to thirty men and women also lost its religious importance. By the time Spanish explorers arrived on the islands, the natives had only a vague recollection of the ritual. They played for the betting and for the prizes offered by local chiefs.

The Caribbean game, like other court games of the New World, traces its origin to the Maya. But where did the Maya themselves come from? And did they bring the game with them or did they invent it after they settled in the Yucatan and its neighboring lands?

No one can answer these questions. But one theory suggests that the Maya originated in the Amazon Valley of South America. Rubber can easily be extracted from trees there, and early explorers found natives there playing a game with a rubber ball. Rules of the game banned the use of the hands.

Other cultural traits of the Maya, including art forms and perhaps language patterns, suggest a link with Amazon peoples, but so far no solid evidence has been found to show where the Maya originated.

And what of their game? Although the great Mayan civilization ended well before the Spanish conquest, the court game never really died out.

One of the things Columbus brought home from the New World was a game played on a court with a rubber ball.

Although Columbus undoubtedly saw natives playing this game, he apparently did not learn exactly how it was played. But he brought home enough information to inspire invention.

With what they had learned from Columbus, the Spanish began playing a game with ball and baskets on a three-sided court. The baskets, shaped like scoops and fitted to the throwing arm, propelled the ball with great speed.

The game became extremely popular among the Spanish Basques, and from Spain the game traveled back to the New World. Jai-alai, as it is called, is popular today in the Caribbean and Central America as well as the Basque district of Spain.

Certainly jai-alai is different from the Mayan game that preserved good over evil. But doesn't the sun still rise, the moon still set? The two games can't be too different.

Chapter Fourteen

Polo

While armored knights were trying to unseat each other on the lists, Eastern horsemen were inventing a remarkable game.

Polo not only demands communication and cooperation among individual players, but it also demands full communication and cooperation between man and beast.

A well-matched horse and rider are a beauty to watch. They represent a level of skill and training attained in few other sports.

Strangely, polo did not arrive in England until soldiers brought it home from India in 1871, and by then the game had all but died out in the East, the land of its origins.

The beginnings of polo are linked both with the development of horsemanship and the evolution of the horse itself. Indeed, it's fair to say that today's domestic horse might not be quite the same animal if it had not been for polo.

Although just two of them survived into historical times, there were apparently several species of wild horse.

Generally, they were poor creatures, either too weak to haul loads of any consequence or too nervous to be managed. But they did interbreed. And by selective breeding, men were able to develop the good qualities and discourage the bad.

The first written mention of riding a horse is preserved on a clay tablet written about 1900 B.C., by Zimri-Lin, King of Mari in Mesopotamia. But the domestic horse was developed much earlier. We do not know when, but it seems that the horse was herded and tamed soon after cattle were domesticated some six thousand years ago.

The first people to make use of the horse lived in the high country bordering the Black and Caspian Seas. They spoke an Indo-European or Aryan language, and were nomads moving frequently in search of fresh pasture for their animals.

In the beginning horses may have been kept only for their milk and meat, but the animals' potential for work must have soon become evident. Scholars still cannot agree how the horse was first put to work. Was it ridden or did it pull a plow or wagon? All we know for certain is that the horse first made its mark in history as a draft animal, pulling a war chariot. Perhaps because dry years had destroyed much of their pasture lands in about 1700 B.C., Aryan horsemen migrated by the thousands into the fertile valleys of the Tigris and Euphrates.

Any armed opposition to their migration was quickly overwhelmed by their horse-drawn chariots. As long as the Aryans had a monopoly on the chariot, they moved east and west as well as south with little opposition. They reached Egypt about 1580 B.C. By then, however, a defense had been discovered. The way to stop a chariot was with another chariot. The horse had thus become vital to all armies of the civilized world.

In hilly country where chariots could not go, the mounted soldier armed with a composite bow took over as the instrument of attack.

Although horsemen in North Africa could turn and stop their horses with taps of a light stick, it was more common in other areas to use a bridle and reins. Bits and curb straps improved the rider's control even more, and saddles kept weight off the horse's spine, which made long distance journeys more comfortable for horse and rider. With these developments came improved skill and knowledge. The Greeks were perhaps the first to raise horsemanship to a science.

Horse and chariot racing, as we have seen, were important events in the Olympic games and other festivals, but the steep terrain of Greece was hardly suited for chariots, let alone racing.

Greek hunters and mounted soldiers became expert cross-country riders who knew how to get the best out of their horses. Training in horsemanship, including jumping, was an important part of the young Greek's education. And every youth was guided by a practical training manual.

Written by Zenophon, the general and historian who lived from about 430 to 354 B.C., the manual brings together common sense and horse sense. It remains today an outstanding guide to horsemanship.

Greeks loved to hunt on horseback, chasing down the quarry until it could be killed with a spear. Zenophon said that hunting was the best training for both horse and rider, recommending it "wherever suitable country and wild beasts exist."

Although Greeks were at home on horseback they did not invent polo, nor did other expert riders of the day. The Scythians, Sarmatians, and similar nomadic tribes practically lived in their saddles, and when not fighting, they apparently spent most of their spare time hunting. Expert as they were, none of these people could have played polo because stirrups had not yet been invented.

The invention is credited to the Huns, the nomadic horsemen who populated the vast lands between China and the Caspian Sea. This land, too poor for farming, sometimes did not even provide enough grazing land for horses. Often it was necessary to migrate great distances to find adequate pasture. Some migrations led the Huns all the way to Europe.

First mention of the stirrup comes from the biography of a Chinese officer who wrote in about 477 A.D. The stirrup made mounting and dismounting much easier and allowed riders to go faster and farther with more comfort. Stirrups also gave the rider increased stability for more accurate arrow shooting and a firmer foundation for handling a lance or swinging a sword. It is odd that the stirrup was the last significant improvement to be made in the horseman's equipment.

The Hun's invention traveled rapidly. It was seen everywhere these restless raiders went. Persian horsemen, who knew the Huns as old enemies, were among the first to adopt the stirrup. And it was soon after this adoption that polo began.

The Persian Empire, which extended at one time from Egypt and the shores of the *Aegean* all the way to India, influenced eastern culture long after it was conquered by Alexander. Thus, when Persian horsemen began playing a ball game the neighbors became interested.

The Byzantine Empire adopted polo from the Persians about the time that the Olympic Games were fading into oblivion. In fact, Theodosius II, the ruler who banned the Olympic Games, is credited with laying out the first polo grounds at Constantinople.

A Persian painting suggests that polo might have been slow-moving and polite in its early days. Certainly a player could not hit the ball very fast or far with the light sticks shown.

The field, not far from the church of Hagia Sophia, overlooked the Sea of Marmara.

Competition among naked athletes was pagan to the early Christians, but they had no objections to polo. Today, however, we would think Byzantine polo cruel.

Numbers on a side were not specified. Collisions were common, and both players and horses suffered injuries that were sometimes fatal. The game was played with a leather ball struck with sticks. And because riders often dropped their sticks, each was followed by a slave on foot whose job it was to resupply his master.

It was tough luck for any slave who could not keep clear of the charging ponies. He was simply run down.

Players lamented the loss of a favorite slave, but such losses did not keep the game from continuing.

In China, polo was introduced as a necessity. Not horsemen by nature or need, the Chinese soldier had to learn to ride in order to fight the Huns.

Hun raids on China were legendary. The nomads were sure to attack whenever China's defenses grew weak. The Huns sometimes drove deep into Chinese territory, forcing the emperor to accept humbling peace terms. The only way to prevent such costly invasions was to maintain a strong cavalry.

Larger horses were imported from India and Persia

and polo was adopted as a training game. The Chinese gentlemen-soldiers gave up their traditional long robes for the more practical blouse and trousers. Black leather caps completed the outfit for polo.

Soon the game grew popular for its own sake. Polo teams were formed everywhere. A man had to belong to a team to have any social status in his community. Women also took to the game with enthusiasm. Teams of women riders were as good as the men and often beat them.

Early in the Sung Dynasty (960 to 1279 A.D.) polo replaced a form of football as the army's official training exercise. Emperor T'ai Tsung (976 to 998 A.D.), one of the game's greatest advocates, codified the rules of polo and ordered national competition every three months. Night games were played under torchlight during T'ai Tsung's reign.

Whenever a game was played before the emperor, he opened the action by throwing the ball onto the field. These games were between the team of the east which wore yellow and the team of the west which wore purple. The goals were marked by poles about ten feet high that were set in stone sockets at each end of the field. Brightly colored banners and golden dragons fluttered from the poles.

The start of play was greeted with loud music from the court band. And a gong was struck three times whenever a goal was scored.

Each team began with a row of twelve flags placed at the side of the field. Whenever a team scored a goal, one of its flags was carried to the emperor's pavilion. The first team to transfer all twelve of its flags was the winner.

Under this system, a game could last several hours, and there were frequent time outs to rest or change ponies. The riders themselves paused for refreshments every time three goals had been scored.

An account of the Persian version of polo was recorded in 1613 by English traveler Sir William Sherley after a visit with the King of Persia.

"Before the house there was a very fair place to the quantity of some ten acres of ground, made very plain: so the King went down, and when he had taken his horse, the drums and trumpets sounded; there was twelve horsemen in all with the King; so they divided themselves into six on one side, and six on the other, having in their hands long rods of wood, about the bigness of a man's finger, and on the end of the rods a piece of wood nailed on like a hammer.

"After they were divided and turned face to face, there came one in the middle, and did throw a wooden ball between both of the companies, and having goals made at either end of the plain, they began their sport, striking the ball with their rods from one to the other, in the fashion of our football play here in England; and ever when the King had gotten the ball before him, the drums and trumpets would play an alarum, and many times the King would come to Sir Anthony [another English visitor] at the window, and ask him how did he like the sport."

Sir William's account, remarkable alone for its long sentences, is also the first description of polo by a westerner. He noted the difficulty of the game, but said that the horses moved after the ball like cats.

It was polo with eight on a side that was taken up by British soldiers who were stationed in India. The first polo club was formed in the Manipur district in 1859. Many others followed, and the game was soon being played by British troops throughout India.

A game in Hurlingham introduced polo to England in 1871. Its popularity grew rapidly, particularly after 1873, when it was reduced to five players on a side. In 1882, it

Modern polo with just four horsemen on a side is so fast and demanding that horses are rested every seven-and-a-half minutes.

was reduced again to four players on a side. These changes speeded up the action, making polo more attractive as a spectator sport.

Play was divided into seven-and-a-half-minute periods or chukkers, with a match consisting of four or six chukkers. So fast is the action of modern polo that riders usually change ponies after one or two chukkers. Unfortunately, the need to feed, care for, and train a string of ponies makes polo an expensive game.

Its growth in the United States stopped with the Great Depression, and although it is still played here and in England and Argentina, polo will never enjoy the widespread popularity it had in ancient times.

A F T E R W O R D

Some say that we are a nation of sports addicts, that we distort our lives by overemphasizing sports, and that we do not give enough attention to the future of mankind and other such serious matters because we think too much about athletic events.

It's all probably true. But should we worry about it?

Just a brief look at ancient cultures and ancient people is enough to tell us that interest in sports is basic to the human character. If for some reason this interest should be suppressed or if it should just falter, then there might well indeed be something wrong. It is then that we should worry.

Meanwhile, by participating and by following sports, we carry on the firm traditions of our ancestors. We do the natural thing. And like others since the dawn of history, we have fun doing it.

What could possibly be wrong with that?

B I B L I O G R A P H Y

Books:

CHENEVIX-TRENCH, CHARLES. *A History of Horsemanship.* Garden City, NY: Doubleday & Co., Inc., 1970.

CULIN, STEWART. *Games of North American Indians.* New York: Dover Publications, Inc., 1975.

DOLAN, EDWARD F., JR. *The Complete Beginner's Guide to Skating.* Garden City, NY: Doubleday & Co., Inc., 1974.

FROST, R. B., editor. *Encyclopedia of Physical Education, Fitness, and Sports.* Reading, MA: Addison-Wesley Publishing Co., Inc., 1971.

GARDINER, E. NORMAN. *Athletics of the Ancient World.* London: Oxford University Press, 1930.

GUTTMAN, ALLEN. *From Ritual to Record, the Nature of Modern Sport.* New York: Columbia University Press, 1979.

HARRIS, H. A. *Sport in Greece and Rome.* Ithaca. NY: Cornell University Press, 1972.

KAREN, RUTH. *Song of the Quail, the Wondrous World of the Maya.* New York: Four Winds Press, 1972.

LÜSCHEN, GÜNTHER. *The Cross-Cultural Analysis of Sports and Games. Champaign,* IL: Stipes Publishing Co., 1970.

LYTTLE, RICHARD B. *The Complete Beginner's Guide to Skiing.* Garden City, NY: Doubleday and Co., Inc., 1978.

MENKE, FRANKE G. The Encyclopedia of Sports. New York: A. S. Barnes & Co., 1963.

MURRELL, JOHN. *Athletics, Sports, and Games.* Winchester, MA: Allen & Unwin, Inc., 1975.

POPE, SAXTON. *Hunting with the Bow and Arrow.* New York: G. P. Putnam's Sons, 1947.

SNOW, DEAN. *The Archeology of North America.* New York: The Viking Press, 1979.

STIERLIN, HENRI. *The Pre-Colombian Civilizations.* New York: Sunflower Books, 1979.

UMMINGER, WALTER. *Supermen, Heroes, and Gods.* London: Thames and Hudson, 1963.

ZEIGLER, EARLE F., editor. *The History of Physical Education and Sports.* New York: Prentice-Hall, Inc., 1979.

Periodicals:

HILDEBRAND, J. R. "The Geography of Games." Washington, D.C., *The National Geographic Magazine,* August, 1919.

HORNBLOWER, G. D. "Wrestling: India and Egypt," New York, *Man,* April, 1928.

MOONEY, JAMES. "The Cherokee Ball Play," Washington, D.C. *The American Anthropologist,* April, 1890.

SIPES, RICHARD G. "War, Sports, and Aggression: An Empirical Test of Two Rival Theories," Washington, D.C. *The American Anthropologist,* February, 1973.

I N D E X